BENEATH THE PROMISE

An Inquiry into India's Socio- Political Landscape

P V INNIYA

Clever Fox® PUBLISHING

Chennai • Bangalore

CLEVER FOX PUBLISHING
Chennai, India

Published by CLEVER FOX PUBLISHING 2025

Paperback ISBN: 978-93-6707-345-2
Hardback ISBN: 978-93-6707-332-2

Cover & Design: Suraksha Srinivasan

Author Contact: afa2024allforall@gmail.com

"Dedicated to every voice that rises in pursuit of equality and justice."

"சமத்துவமும் சிந்தனையும் மட்டுமே
என் உரிமையின் அடையாளம்."

– PV Inniya

Dedication

To every soul who has endured injustice, inequality, and silence—

This book is for you.

To the leaders who lit the path before us—Thanthai Periyar, Dr. B.R. Ambedkar, Karl Marx, and Thalaivar Kalaignar — for rising against the tide of injustice, for dreaming of an equal world, and for giving us the language to question, resist, and hope.

We have not reached the destination yet,
but we march forward — through their thoughts, through their fire.

To Thalaivar Kalaignar,
who has been the starting point of my ideological journey since childhood. It was through him that I first entered this world of thought — only after him did I explore other leaders and ideologies.

To Kanimozhi Ma'am,
Your presence, your words, have been my constant strength and an anchor through every storm. You are the living proof that conviction and compassion can co-exist with power and grace — that one can stand firm for justice without ever losing tenderness for people. In you, I see not just a leader, but a guiding light whose courage gives me hope, and whose humility teaches me how to walk with dignity. I have grown seeing you — not in your shadow, but in the radiance of your guiding light. Your words have always reached me at the moments I needed them most, bringing calm in my restlessness and courage in my doubts, urging me to move forward on the path I have chosen. I carry an endless love and respect for you, one that words can never fully capture. To me, you are not just an inspiration — you are a quiet force that shapes who I strive to become, every single day.

To Asiriyar K. Veeramani Ayya,

Who has been a great support to both me and this book from our very first meeting.
Ayya, you have shown how deeply you value young minds and their work. Thank you for being an immense guide and a powerful inspiration to all of us.

To Arulmozhi Ma'am,
Your gracious presence and encouragement have strengthened my journey in unimaginable ways.

To my parents, family, and friends – your love, faith, and unwavering support have been the pillars on which I stand. You have been my anchor through storms and my wind when I needed to fly. To the quiet strength and love that holds me steady, even in the moments no one else sees – you are the reason I keep moving forward, the heartbeat behind every step I take. To every person who believed in me, who guided me, who stood silently beside me without needing words – thank you.

This book lives because of all of you, and within its pages, so does a piece of my heart.

CONTENTS

WORDS OF ENDORSMENT

DRAVIDAR KAZHAGAM

Head Quarters : Periyar Thidal, 84/1 (50), E.V.K.Sampath Road, Vepery, Chennai-600 007. Tamil Nadu, INDIA
• Phone : 91-44-26618161 / 62 / 63 • Fax: 91-44-26618866
• E-mail: dkheadquarters@gmail.com • Website: www.dravidarkazhagam.org

Founder President
Thanthai Periyar

President
K.Veeramani, M.A.,B.L.,

Date :

11.08.2025

FOREWORD

"Beneath the Promise" by Ms.P.V.Inniya has included almost all the progressive thoughts of Thanthai Periyar, the unparalleled social revolutionary. Stress has been laid on castes that have rooted deeply in the political life of India. Inspite of its centuries old foundation, caste continues to imprint on the governance now in existence. The simplicity, lucidity and brevity in her writing are praiseworthy. She has rightly chosen an apt title for her book. It clearly implies that the promise of the Indian Constitution has not yet been kept and so we are all suffering on a lower level of existence; below its promise.

The author has taken pain with perseverance at such a young age to bring out a thought – provoking book, useful to everyone who aspire a truly egalitarian, casteless society. Her work is without obscurity and needless complex expressions. This book would certainly be a source of inspiration for young writers to contribute something new, to the already existing fund of knowledge in Periyar thought.

The author rightly says that we are all bound by the invisible chains of caste even after seventy eight years of freedom. We still struggle restlessly to eradicate social inequality, gender bias, religious bias, social injustice, superstitions and dehumanisation. She stresses that the only solution for the problem of societal divisions is equality that could be caused only by unity of our people. It has been highlighted in this book that there is diversity everywhere in everything, but castes become a problem only when diversity is transformed into discrimination.

The author says freedom is not a privilege for women; it is their birth right. Thanthai Periyar condemned gender inequality in society and raised voice against the enslavement of women and male dominance. His voice has echoed in the expressions of the author in the chapter revolving around societal inequality.

Stalwarts like Thanthai Periyar, Babasaheb Ambedkar and Jyotirao Phule fought always against the evils of caste. By the impact of their services

DRAVIDAR KAZHAGAM

Head Quarters : Periyar Thidal, 84/1 (50), E.V.K.Sampath Road, Vepery, Chennai-600 007. Tamil Nadu, INDIA

- Phone : 91-44-26618161 / 62 / 63 • Fax: 91-44-26618866
- E-mail: dkheadquarters@gmail.com • Website: www.dravidarkazhagam.org

Founder President
Thanthai Periyar

President
K.Veeramani, M.A.,B.L.,

Date :

the world is far better today compared to how it was in the past, but the discriminations have not vanished entirely and hence the transformation is not complete. We still have a long way to go because caste is an omnipresent practice. She has explained all these clearly, insisting on the dire need of a casteless India.

The author quotes the opening words in the preamble of the Indian Constitution: "We, the People of India"...... and specifies all the five key political principles – sovereignty, socialism, secularism, democracy and republicanism. She is quite right when she says that democracy is meaningless without social justice and that Reservations are meant to break the centuries old chains of inequality.

Bertrand Russel used to say that Indian authors enjoy quoting several other authors instead of expressing their own ideas. But we can proudly say that Thanthai Periyar never quoted anybody in his works. He used to express his original thoughts at all times. I find this admirable quality in the author of this book. She has merely used the principles of great Stalwarts in support of her arguments.

The author insists on the role of educational institutions in eradicating caste based discriminations. She refers to Couplet No.972 in 'Thirukkural' where Thiruvalluvar states that all are equal by birth. She hails Thanthai Periyar as the crusader for education. She praises him as "a revolution in human form".

In my foreword, I would like to move forward and conclude with just a four-word comment on this book – **"PROGRESSIVE THOUGHTS - PERFECTLY BROUGHT".**

(K. VEERAMANI)
President

கனிமொழி கருணாநிதி
Kanimozhi Karunanidhi
Member of Parliament
Lok Sabha
Thoothukkudi Constituency - Tamil Nadu

26, Dr. Rajendra Prasad Road,
New Delhi - 110001
Telefax : 011-23782887
E-mail : kanimozhimds@gmail.com

46/1, Prashanthi Apartments,
2nd Cross Street, C.I.T. Colony,
Mylapore, Chennai-600 004 (T.N.)
Tel. : 044-24670606
Fax : 044-24670001

21.08.2025

Chennai

Foreword

I would like to extend my sincere congratulations on the forthcoming publication of Iniya's debut book 'Beneath the Promise- An inquiry into India's Socio- Political landscape'. Releasing first book is a remarkable accomplishment, and addressing such a nuanced and significant subject reflects her intellectual rigor and courage.

Caste is a subject that is often spoken about in hushed tones or with academic detachment, yet it affects lives with undeniable force every single day. What makes this book different is not only its clarity and courage, but the voice behind it: a young woman, bold enough to question, empathetic enough to listen.

This is her first book—but it reads like the work of someone who has walked many miles through history. She does not approach the subject as a detached observer, nor does she rely on outrage alone. Instead, she blends research, personal insight, and lived narratives with a rare sensitivity, revealing the intricate ways in which caste operates—in schools, in marriages, in neighbourhoods.

Dravidian ideology is rooted against the caste-based discrimination and focussing on building inclusive society. From Periyar, Perarignar Anna to

கனிமொழி கருணாநிதி
Kanimozhi Karunanidhi
Member of Parliament
Lok Sabha
Thoothukkudi Constituency • Tamil Nadu

सत्यमेव जयते

26, Dr. Rajendra Prasad Road,
New Delhi - 110001
Telefax : 011-23782887
E-mail : kanimozhimds@gmail.com

46/1, Prashanthi Apartments,
2nd Cross Street, C.I.T. Colony,
Mylapore, Chennai-600 004 (T.N.)
Tel : 044-24670606
Fax : 044-24670001

Thalaivar Kalaignar, our leaders strived to achieve social justice in all aspects of life from education, job opportunities to marriages. Various initiatives like reservations, supported the marginalised and oppressed people to move forward in life. But even in progressive states like Tamil Nadu repercussions of caste system still prevail. Incidents like honour killings continue to happen even nowadays.

Apart from stringent laws, political representation, education, and economic empowerment, changing social attitudes and challenging caste-based prejudices will require sustained efforts to promote empathy and understanding.

In a field where diverse voices are essential, her contribution as a young woman author is both timely and necessary. I have no doubt that her work will offer fresh perspectives and foster meaningful dialogue within the broader political discourse.

Wishing the author a great success with the publication and the many opportunities that will surely follow.

With Best Wishes,

Kanimozhi Karunanidhi

Constituency : 102F/20M, 6th Street, Kurinji Nagar, Polpettai, Thoothukkudi-628002. Tamil Nadu • Tel.: 0461- 2348101

A deep study of the age old disease and in search of a remedy .

Inniya PV, a student of law has emerged as a potential researcher through her project titled 'Beneath The Promise'. I am glad that I got the opportunity to read it.

Inniya has taken the task of tracing the roots of the 'Caste' through the Socio Political Landscape of India.

She identified the source from Pusushasuktha of Rg Veda which was concretised by the law of Manu and the influence of Manu Smrithi passing through ages.

Inniya has narrated the incidents of murder, rape and assault on the individuals, families and communities of suppressed classes from various parts of India. She explains how such crimes play a major role in depriving the dignity of human life to the depressed classes and demoralising them from getting organised and fighting against the oppression.

Inniya places the theory of equality from the Thirukkural ' Pirappokkum ella uyirkkum' meaning 'All are equal by birth' as an anti thesis to the inequality prescribed by Manu's Varnasrama dharma.

She has given a vivid picture about the struggles of the great reformer and revolutionary Jyothirao Phule and Savithri bai Phule, the constructive contributions of Dr. B. R. Ambedkar ,and Periyar E V Ramasamy. She rightly describes Dr. Ambedkar as The architect of Social Justice and Periyar EV Ramasamy as The crusader for Social Justice.

The obscurity and complexity of the caste system has been exposed with historical data and the changes brought in by social struggles and by the Constitutional provisions are well documented.

Inniya concludes the research with her positive suggestions to move forward from the caste based inequality to a civilised society.

The change in the social psyche without which the claims of the human race as superior to other living beings are beautifully illustrated by Iniya.

Congratulations to Inniya and my wishes for her to continue her journey in seeking justice to the oppressed people .

A. Arulmozhi
Advocate of Madras Highcourt.(37 years of Experience)
Media Secretary of Dravidar Kazhagam

Being a part of an eye-opening discipline – Journalism, I often look for the purpose of 'headlines', their behind stories and justice. Reading the book, Beneath the Promise: An Inquiry into India's Socio- Political Landscape helps me understand on a point, how caste isn't just a social structure—it's a living reality that shapes elections, policies, and everyday experiences in ways we don't always acknowledge. It also sheds light on the nation's constitutional diplomacy and the tireless efforts of our foreleaders—on the grounds and in the assembly over years, ensuring fair representation.

What stays with me most is how the book deals with caste hierarchy—not just as a fact, but as something constantly contested through law, protest, and politics. It reminded me that the Constitution is not just a legal document— it's also a promise, one that's still being argued over in the parliament debates, courtrooms, and street protests. The section on caste hierarchy and political representation was especially powerful. It pushed me to reflect on how stories are framed in today's media—whose voices get amplified, and whose struggles remain invisible.

This book reminds me of the responsibility we practice when reporting on caste and democracy. It doesn't preach, but it pushes us to think harder, ask better questions, and stay with the discomfort of complex truths. I believe this creation has the power to spark a more inclusive mindset and encourage rational progress; Let the change emerge from our own minds.

PRITHVI S
B. Voc., Digital Journalism
Loyola College, Chennai.

Beneath the Promise offered me a profound and nuanced window into India's socio-political landscape — one I previously understood only through academic texts and media coverage. The book's in-depth exploration of caste dynamics, constitutional contradictions, and representational gaps illuminated the deep-rooted complexities shaping modern India. I was particularly struck by how the author balances rigorous legal-political analysis with lived experiences and ethical reflection. As an international student, the narrative challenged my preconceptions and made me more conscious of how structural inequalities persist even in democracies. It made me reflect on the global nature of marginalisation and the importance of culturally grounded scholarship. This work is not just informative; it's humanising. It calls on all of us — wherever we're from — to re-evaluate the promises our societies make, and for whom they are truly.

Emily Thompson
MSc International Relations
University of Oxford

I particularly found the chapter on 'Indian Constitution and Caste' informative, yet practical. The chapter presents a clear and insightful analysis of the caste system in India, rooted in on-ground realities. By weaving in real-world examples, it brings abstract concepts to life and highlights how caste continues to shape social dynamics in both rural and urban contexts. The explanation of the reservation system is particularly effective, simple yet nuanced, emphasizing the crucial distinction between equity and equality without oversimplifying the issue. In doing so, it challenges prevailing misconceptions and encourages a more informed understanding of affirmative action policies. The chapter also stands out for offering thoughtful, actionable solutions to address caste-based discrimination. Its interdisciplinary approach, drawing from sociology, political science, and contemporary policy discourse, makes it not just informative but solution-oriented. A valuable read for anyone seeking to understand caste beyond textbooks and to engage with the systemic dimensions of social justice in India.

With regards,

S Krishna Priya.
MA English Literature(Prof)

As a practising junior lawyer at the Madras High Court, I found this work both thought-provoking and deeply relevant to contemporary legal and social discourse in India. The author's analysis of caste, constitutional principles, and political realities is meticulously researched and presented in a manner that is both accessible and intellectually engaging. What stands out most is the balanced approach — combining legal interpretation with historical and sociological insights — making this book a valuable resource for law students, legal practitioners, and anyone seeking to understand the complex intersection of caste and politics in India. This is a commendable contribution to legal literature.

Anu Priya
B.com llb
Junior Advocate

Before reading Beneath the Promise, politics and caste felt like distant concepts that had little to do with my field. But this book showed me how deeply they influence every aspect of our society, from education to opportunity. I was struck by the way Inniya brings historical context and personal accounts together to make complex issues understandable without losing their depth. It pushed me to reflect on how privilege shapes the paths we walk, often invisibly. As a student of technology, it reminded me that progress isn't just about innovation - it's about ensuring that the benefits of change reach everyone.

Rahul Narayanan

INTRODUCTION

Thozhar Inniya approached me to write a review for her book, "Beneath the Promise: An Inquiry into India's Socio-Political Landscape." As I began reading, I sensed that this was a substantial research work, given the depth and breadth of the subject it addresses. Before reaching the halfway mark, I messaged Thozhar Inniya to thank her for choosing me to review this remarkable book.

I have been reading extensively on social justice and caste annihilation for over a decade. My readings have included works by social justice leaders and stalwarts like Dr. Ambedkar, Thanthai Periyar, Dr. T.M. Nair, Peraringar Anna, Dr. Kalaingar, Perasiriyar Anbalagan, and Aasiriyar K. Veeramani. However, when it comes to contemporary writings that explore caste issues in a deeper and broader context for the modern reader, I found a gap in recent literature. I occasionally referred to Isabel Wilkerson's *Caste*, which discusses the American context by linking racism with casteism.

Thozhar Inniya's *"Beneath the Promise"* fills that void, providing valuable insights into the caste realities of India today. The book is accessible to both novices and experts. Its elegant and straightforward language makes it not just a scholarly work but also a compelling literary read.

> *For outsiders who are unfamiliar with India and how its democracy functions, this book provides a clear and insightful overview.*

> *For those interested in politics and seeking to understand caste, the reservation system, the Indian Constitution, and the laws surrounding social justice, electoral politics, and the role of caste — this book covers all these topics, offering a broader perspective on contemporary India.*
>
> *For researchers or avid readers of social justice issues, this book will be a valuable addition to their bookshelf for quick reference and makes an excellent gift.*

The book begins by exploring the roots of the issue, explaining the concept of caste and its foundation. It details how caste was created to establish the dominance of brahmins and how it was rendered invincible through religious texts, which falsely proclaimed that caste was divinely ordained. The author quotes Dr. Ambedkar's scholarly writings extensively, providing greater historical context and a deeper understanding of the subject.

The significance of this book also lies in its extensive use of facts, case studies, and documentation of atrocities against Dalits at both the ground level and within institutions. These serve as concrete evidence and stand as a powerful statement against caste-based discrimination in present-day India.

The author emphasizes the importance of the reservation system, illustrating how it has helped the downtrodden—particularly backward and scheduled castes—to improve their lives. However, she also questions the caste-based identities themselves and the problems that often accompany them.

Inniya envisions a society where everyone is equal, and no one is identified by caste. She advocates for equal opportunities for all to dream and thrive. This is not a utopian dream—she maintains that with continuous effort and a shift in mindset, such a society is achievable.

Her writing goes beyond mere statements or opinions; Inniya keeps questioning and encourages readers to think independently and critically about these issues.

Several places in this book gave me a wow factor. One such instance is how the author has beautifully linked the Classic Tamil Literature "Thirukkural" and the foundations of the Indian Constitution with the concept of equality.

The book delves deeply into the Indian Constitution—its importance in keeping democracy alive in India, and the constitutional articles that safeguard equality, diversity, equal opportunity, minority rights, and more.

At the same time, the author does not shy away from highlighting the challenges in implementing specific laws in India. For example, even though manual scavenging was officially prohibited under the 2013 Act, the harsh truth is that it continues to exist in practice.

Similarly, despite strict laws against caste discrimination, the country has witnessed tragic institutional murders, such as the death of Rohith Vemula, a Dalit PhD scholar at the University of Hyderabad.

The author also points out how corruption disproportionately impacts Dalits—while they are constitutionally promised reservation and representation, large-scale manipulation continues in education and government job recruitments. A striking example of this is the Vyapam scam in Madhya Pradesh.

The book also explores the lives and contributions of prominent leaders such as Dr. Ambedkar, Thanthai Periyar, Mahatma Gandhi, Perarignar Anna, Kalaingar Karunanidhi, and Ram Manohar Lohia. It extends its scope to international figures like Nelson Mandela, Karl Marx, and Che Guevara, highlighting their struggles for the oppressed. Additionally, the book briefly discusses political parties like DMK and BSP and their work in social justice movements. This provides a comprehensive perspective for anyone seeking guidance on social justice politics.

Inniya delves deeply into the analysis of various elections across India and explores the role of caste in these electoral processes. She examines the complexities of caste dynamics in vote bank politics, illustrating how caste is both a tool for identity, representation, and a means of empowerment.

I would like to mention some key points I highlighted while reading the book. This should offer a brief overview of the topics covered in the book:

- Reservation is about *compensation*, not *privilege*. It's about giving those who have been historically oppressed a chance to catch up.
- So when people say, "Reservation isn't needed anymore," I challenge them: "Are we really equal now, or are we just pretending because it's more comfortable?
- Here's an interesting point: reservation doesn't just help the direct beneficiaries. It helps *everyone*. Think about it—when marginalized individuals enter the workforce or get an education, they don't just uplift themselves; they enrich society with new perspectives, skills, and experiences. They break cycles of poverty and ignorance, making society more dynamic and forward-thinking.
- Reservation is not about *privilege*. It's about *correcting an imbalance* that has been in place for centuries. It's about providing everyone with a *real shot* at success. And until we build a society where every single person has the same opportunity, it remains the necessary step forward.
- Let's be clear: caste is not just a relic of the past; it is a living, breathing structure that adapts, that persists, that fights to stay relevant even when the law says it shouldn't. If it were truly gone, why do Dalit students still drop out of schools at higher rates due to discrimination? Why do manual scavengers—those forced into inhumane labor for

centuries—still exist despite legal bans? Why do we still hear of caste-based violence, honor killings, and social boycotts? If the Constitution was enough on its own, then why do these injustices remain a daily reality for so many?

- The truth is, no Constitution, however powerful, can single-handedly erase centuries of conditioning. The law can dictate rights, but it cannot dictate mindsets. That is a battle that must be fought within every home, every school, every workplace, and every conversation. It is a battle that demands uncomfortable discussions, challenges to privilege, and a willingness to see beyond our own lived experiences.
- What these legislative efforts reveal is a deep and ongoing struggle: while the Constitution may light the path, the journey toward equality requires collective societal will. Caste is not merely a legal problem to be solved in courtrooms; it is a social reality entrenched in mindsets, habits, and hierarchies. That is where the true test lies—not in whether laws exist, but in whether they are allowed to work, and whether we, as a people, are ready to confront what still holds us back.
- There's a remarkable moment I want to highlight. Ambedkar, after drafting the Constitution, went on record saying that **equality** is the "first and the most important" principle for any nation.
- As I think about the **Constitution's vision of equality**, I can't help but feel the resonance with Thiruvalluvar's profound words. In many ways, his teachings were a roadmap, guiding the leaders of modern India in their struggle to create a just and fair society.
- It's easy to admire Gandhi's commitment to social justice, but I can't help but wonder — could his message have been more radical? Could he have envisioned a society completely free from caste-based discrimination, rather than trying to "reform" a system that, by its very nature, entrenched inequality?
- As I reflect on Gandhi's life, I'm reminded that reform is never clean or simple. It is often a messy, difficult process that asks us to hold

conflicting truths at the same time. Gandhi's contradictions are part of his greatness. Let's see him as a man — a man who fought for freedom, equality, and justice, but who, like all of us, had to navigate the complex web of his own beliefs, doubts, and contradictions.

- Karunanidhi inherited the mantle from **Annadurai**, but he took it to another level. He wasn't just content with **challenging the Brahminical order**; he sought to **reshape the very fabric of Tamil Nadu**. He embraced the ideals of **social welfare** and **affirmative action**, ensuring that **education and political representation** weren't privileges for the few, but **rights for all**.
- And let's talk about **reservations**, an issue that's still so fiercely debated today. Karunanidhi was unwavering in his belief that **caste-based reservations were essential**. He didn't see them as a means to divide society; instead, he saw them as a **tool for empowerment**—a way to level the playing field for those who had been **historically deprived**.
- We may never know exactly how **Annadurai** or **Karunanidhi** would have tackled today's political climate, but one thing is clear: **their fight for justice wasn't about personal gain**—it was about lifting those who had been forgotten for so long. And that fight continues today.
- This is the struggle of the story — a society striving for progress, yet hindered by its past, where the shackles of caste remain firmly in place. The question now is whether India can break free from these divisions and move toward a future where politics is truly about people, not about the labels society has placed upon them.
- Identity-based policies, which the Constitution sought to balance through social justice mechanisms, have evolved within democratic politics. While electoral democracy has provided marginalized communities a platform for representation, it has also led to competitive identity politics.
- The next time you hear someone say that Indian democracy is the world's largest, remember: it is also one of the most complex. Because here,

elections are not just about governance—they are about aspirations, representation, and the evolving nature of political consciousness.

- For many from these communities, this wasn't just about representation—it was a lifeline—a chance to break free from centuries of silence and start contributing to a democratic society. Over the decades, this system has played a key role in bringing people from these marginalized communities into the corridors of power. They have been able to raise issues that affect them, from education to healthcare to rural development, putting the spotlight on their unique struggles. But, even with all this, there's always the question: *Has this been enough?* Are we truly seeing empowerment, or is it just a token presence in the political space?
- Despite digital progress, India's political fabric remains deeply embedded in social hierarchies, making it crucial to ensure that technology doesn't exacerbate existing inequalities. Recent state elections have showcased this duality, where social media campaigns, such as those in Tamil Nadu and Uttar Pradesh, have successfully elevated governance-based narratives alongside identity politics. Yet, issues like caste-based reservation and religious divides continue to influence voting patterns significantly.
- Here's where the future of Indian democracy lies: It's in bridging the gap between caste-based mobilization and universal social progress. I want to bring you back to that small town in Uttar Pradesh, where the voices of political leaders are intertwined with caste, but there's something else happening, something you don't hear in the speeches. The youth of these communities are no longer just looking for representation; they are looking for opportunities. They are asking for policies that will improve healthcare, education, and job prospects, regardless of caste.
- The future of caste in electoral politics isn't about completely removing its influence. It's about **redefining it**—from something that divides to

something that can uplift. We need to ask ourselves: **how do we move from tokenism to true empowerment?** How do we build a society where the benefits of **economic growth**, **social development**, and **education** can transcend caste-based barriers, and where leadership is based on **merit**, **vision**, and **policies** that can address **every citizen's needs**, regardless of background?

- **Equality** should be the guiding principle in shaping our democracy. We are moving towards a time when **no one's potential should be limited by their caste**, and no one should be left behind simply because of where they were born or what their ancestors faced. **Everyone**, regardless of their identity, should have the same chance to thrive, to succeed, and to contribute to the growth of this nation.
- The question isn't just about removing caste from electoral politics—it's about **creating a society where caste doesn't matter anymore**. We must work towards **policies that are centered on merit, capability, and need**, not identity.
- Picture this: an election season where political parties are **competing not for caste votes** but for the **best healthcare policies**, **best educational reforms**, and **most impactful economic opportunities**. This isn't a utopian dream; it's a possible reality. Political campaigns need to shift from identity-based appeals to issue-based campaigns that promise tangible changes. Imagine a voter no longer casting their ballot based on who they are told they should vote for, but based on what matters most to them—whether it's a new hospital in their locality, better roads, or more jobs. **When politics is about the future we can build together, caste stops becoming the focal point.**
- In the end, the future of caste in Indian politics isn't about abolishing it from our discussions—it's about **transforming the political and social system to a place where caste is no longer a factor** in determining someone's worth or their future. Let's focus on **equality**—because, ultimately, **everyone deserves to be equal**.

- This isn't just a matter of policy; it's a matter of our humanity. The fight for equality is not something that can be relegated to law schools or political debates. It's something that must live in our hearts and minds, in our daily actions and words. So, the next time we speak of equality, let us ask ourselves—what does it really mean, and how can we ensure that the promises of the Constitution are not just words on a page, but the reality for every single person, regardless of their caste? Let's stop waiting for a revolution that may never come and start building it—quietly, steadily, in every moment because that's where true change begins.
- Reservations in education and employment were supposed to be a game-changer, right? A system designed to break the centuries-old shackles of caste discrimination and give those from marginalized communities a chance to build a life free from the weight of centuries of oppression. But, as we peel back the layers of this complex issue, we realize that while some doors have been opened, others remain locked, and the journey of true equality feels far from over.
- Yes, the reservation system is a victory—it has opened doors. But we need to ask ourselves, as a society: Are we content with just giving marginalized students a seat at the table, or do we want to create an environment where they can thrive? Are we willing to challenge our biases and offer real support, or are we going to let them fight their battles alone?
- Let's start by asking ourselves: **How do we create a world where every student can thrive, regardless of their background?** It's time we begin that journey—because **equality isn't just a destination; it's a path we must walk together**.
- As Ambedkar said, the Constitution alone cannot free us. It is our mindset that needs to evolve. And that evolution starts with each of us, questioning not only the system but ourselves. It's about asking the difficult questions: *What have I inherited? What do I need to unlearn?*

How can I actively dismantle the systems of inequality I've been part of, even unknowingly? It's a journey of constant self-reflection, of holding ourselves accountable, and of making sure our actions align with our ideals.
- We need to rethink education—not as a luxury reserved for a select few, but as a fundamental right for all. It isn't just about textbooks and classrooms. It's about creating an ecosystem where every child can grow, thrive, and rise beyond the circumstances they were born into. It's about giving every child access to the same opportunities—the kind that build character, nurture dreams, and empower them to break free from the shackles of societal divisions.
- Equality doesn't mean treating everyone the same. It means giving everyone the resources and opportunities they need to thrive.

There are a few sections in the book where Inniya expresses her ideology and how she wishes to identify herself:

If there's one thing I have learned from Periyar, it is this: **self-respect is not a gift—it is taken, seized, and defended at all costs.**

Through the **Self-Respect Movement**, Periyar told people:

- Don't bow to gods who keep you in chains.
- Don't follow customs that treat you as lesser.
- **Don't accept that suffering in this life will reward you in the next.**
- Demand respect. Demand dignity. Demand equality.

I don't just **respect** Periyar—I **carry his fire within me**. His words are not just history; they are **a living force** that shapes the way I see the world.

His **unapologetic rebellion**, his **refusal to conform**, and his **audacity to question what others accepted as fate**—that's what inspires me every day. He didn't just **fight for the oppressed**; he **handed them a**

weapon—the power of rationality, the courage of rebellion, and the conviction of self-respect.

And that's what I take from him.

- Never accept oppression as destiny.
- Never let tradition silence you.
- Never let fear decide your beliefs.

Periyar's refusal to accept the status quo in his time resonates with me every day. He made me question my own complacency and taught me that real change begins when we challenge the very things we have accepted without question. If Periyar has taught me anything, it is this: to think, to challenge, and above all, to never bow down.

Because **self-respect is not given. It is taken.**

This book, in many ways, is a gift to society from Inniya and serves as a call to action towards building a casteless society where everyone gets everything(எல்லாருக்கும் எல்லாம்). In her words: "ALL for ALL."

Please join me in wishing Inniya success with this book and in her life, as she strives to fulfil all her dreams.

Rajarajan RJ B.E.,MBA
Singapore
17-AUG-2025

ABSTRACT (AUTHORS STATEMENT)

Dear gentle readers,

India is a land of stories—of empires and revolutions, of poets and politicians, of unity and division. A country where languages shift as the landscapes do, where cultures intertwine, creating a magnificent tapestry of diversity. And yet, beneath this splendor lies a truth we cannot ignore: caste, an age-old force that continues to shape lives, policies, and politics.

For centuries, caste has been more than just a social construct; it has been a silent architect of inequality, deciding who gets access to education, opportunities, and basic dignity. Today, despite the promises of the Indian Constitution, caste still lingers—not just in rural villages but in bustling cities, in boardrooms, in university admissions, in the very foundations of our democracy. It is whispered in political campaigns, written into policies, and reflected in voting patterns.

This book begins where India's story does—with its socio-political fabric. It unravels the historical roots of caste, its evolution through colonial and post-independence India, and its deep entanglement with governance and law. We will explore how political parties have both challenged and exploited caste, how legal frameworks have attempted to break these barriers, and how far we have truly come in building an equal society.

But this is not merely a study of the past. It is a call to imagine a different future. A future where caste is no longer a barrier, where diversity is a source of strength rather than division. In its final pages, this book will ask the most pressing question—how do we move forward? What must be done to truly unite India beyond caste?

Because in the end, dear gentle readers, the answer is simple yet profound: we are not just members of a caste, a community, or a political vote bank. We are Indians. Only Indians. And it is time we start living like it.

INSIGHTS INTO INDIA AND ITS COMPLEX SOCIAL FABRIC

> *"India is a culmination of diversity woven into its very fabric."*

This book will explore India's deeply entrenched caste design and its political application. India is a mixture of cultures and traditions, and cultures and practices evolve every 100 kilometers. India is known for its cultural heritage and its festivals, geographical boundaries, and diversity can't be forgotten.

"Even after 78 years of independence, India is still chained by the invisible walls of caste.

Why?" Despite decades of progress, India continues to grapple with deep-rooted inequalities We have come across 78 years of independence yet the struggle for fundamental rights, be it against social inequality, gender discrimination, or religious bias remains ongoing. in all these factors there is only one prominent cause which is inequality **the ultimate solution for all this is societal divides is equality this can happen only by unity,** How will this transformation unfold? What steps must be taken to dismantle caste-based oppression? These questions will be explored in depth as we progress through this book.

But let us begin with one of the Paramount aspects of India's social fabric; **which is diversity**, India has diversity in everything and everywhere—religion, culture, language, geography—and the list goes on. To name just a few, there is diversity in religion, culture, language, and geography. However, the question arises: Is caste a form of diversity in India? The answer is definitely no. In my opinion, In my opinion, caste becomes problematic when diversity transforms into discrimination. It only becomes an issue when individuals forget the core principle of equality and fail to treat their fellow beings with the dignity and respect they deserve.

Now let us take a look at a Pivotal aspect of India's social fabric, They say caste is a centuries-old practice, so why does this system still cause conflict today? to find the answer,to this we need to know how caste originated and what its roots are. To do this, we must look into the Varna system. What is it? Where did it emerge from? Is it still practiced? And is there even a need to practice it today? Or is there even a need to practice it today?

This varna system

This varna system is highly associated with the Hindu religion. It divides society into four main classifications or "Varnas": Brahmins, Kshatriyas, Vaishyas, and Shudras, ranked from the highest to the lowest. In ancient times, these classifications were primarily based on occupations. Brahmins were priests, scholars, or teachers serving the divine; Kshatriyas were warriors and rulers; Vaishyas were farmers, traders, and merchants; and Shudras were tasked with labor-intensive jobs like street sweeping and cleaning. This system is notably mentioned in the *Manusmriti*. So, when did this system originate? It emerged after the arrival of the Aryans around 1500 BCE.

The Rise of Untouchability

Why is caste a problem? Have you ever thought about it? The root of the issue lies in the practice of untouchability. When higher-caste individuals began to consider the lower castes as "impure," it led to widespread discrimination. Untouchability became a deeply ingrained practice, and the lower castes were treated as less than human. They were denied access to temples, excluded from villages, and forced to live on the outskirts. These injustices created a stark divide, not just socially, but also psychologically, reinforcing the belief in inherent superiority and inferiority. Much more about this will be explored in the next chapter.

Religious diversity

But now is caste the only social problem in India? No, it is not. However, caste remains one of the most significant problems that cannot be overlooked. Another crucial element of India's social fabric is religious diversity. India is home to more than seven different religions, and religion plays a central role in the lives of its people. The most practiced religions in India include Hinduism, Buddhism, Sikhism, Christianity, Islam, and Jainism.

India's constitution declares the country as a secular state, meaning there is no state religion, reflecting the nation's religious diversity. Despite this vast religious spectrum, one key lesson we all share is that in every religion, and through every god, we are taught the values of love and compassion for one another.

Among these religions, Hinduism is the largest, with over 79% of the Indian population identifying as Hindus, making it the majority religion. However, even within Hinduism, there is remarkable diversity, just as there is within other religions like Christianity, which includes Catholicism,

Protestantism, Eastern Orthodoxy, and Oriental Orthodoxy. Within Hinduism, you find further distinctions, such as:

- **Vaishnavism**: Worship of Vishnu and his avatars like Rama and Krishna
- **Shaivism**: Worship of Shiva
- **Shaktism**: Worship of the divine feminine (Shakti, Durga, Kali)
- **Smartism**: Worship of multiple deities with a focus on Advaita philosophy

These diverse forms of worship, cultural practices, and traditions vary across regions. For instance, in the northern regions of India, most people worship Lord Krishna and Rama. In the south, deities like Lord Muruga and Meenakshi are more prominent, and these gods are largely not worshiped in the north. In the east, Durga and Kali are central, as seen in places like Puri Jagannath, while in the west, Jainism holds considerable influence.

Despite this vast diversity in beliefs, the unifying factor in Hinduism remains caste, *jati*, or *varna*, which continues to be an inseparable part of its structure. In many ways, everything remains tied to this classification.

Manusmriti

The *Manusmriti*, often referred to as the law book or rule book of Hinduism, is an ancient legal text, also known as the Law of Manu. When discussing the *Manusmriti*, one cannot overlook the landmark protest — the burning of the *Manusmriti*. But before we delve into that, let's first have a brief introduction to Manu. There's no doubt that the *Manusmriti* played a significant role in shaping Hinduism and the lives of its followers.

From a young age, we are taught the difference between right and wrong, what is acceptable and what is not. For instance, if we hurt someone as children, our parents or guardians immediately correct us, reminding us not to repeat the act. This simple lesson, though seemingly basic, is deeply rooted in our generational cultural conditioning, and it ties back to ancient texts like the *Manusmriti*. It doesn't just shape individual behavior, but also dictates the norms for entire communities.

So, why is the *Manusmriti* no longer followed or even considered? This remains a deeply debatable question. The *Manusmriti* contains a systemized framework of inequality, especially with its rigid caste hierarchy, along with profound gender inequality. These elements continue to cast long shadows, remaining largely unspoken and unheard. This is what makes the *Manusmriti* a controversial text.

To analyze India's journey toward equality, one must first confront the texts and traditions that justified inequality in the first place.

The Burning of Manusmriti: A Symbolic Rejection of Caste-Based Oppression

A prominent protest which is the burning of Manusmirthi this protest was held by Dr B R Ambedkar this protest was upheld to make a strong statement against caste-based discrimination, manu had contained discriminatory and inflicting approach to certain societies, to be more particularly to Dalits. We all know Dr has always been taking a stand against discrimination on any basis mostly against Dalits, December 25, 1927, in Maharashtra a place called Mahad this landmarking protest took place Dr along with his followers organized this protest they burned a copy of Manusmriti to symbolize their stand against caste-based discrimination. it was indeed a symbolic rejection of this social hierarchy, This act was not just a symbolic gesture but a powerful statement challenging the deep-rooted social hierarchies that had oppressed marginalized communities, particularly the Dalits, for centuries. The Mahad protest stands as a testament to the courage of those who dared to confront systemic oppression. It was not merely the destruction of a book but the burning of ideas that perpetuated caste-based discrimination, paving the way for the ideals enshrined later in the Indian Constitution—liberty, equality, and fraternity. We will be discussing Dr. B.R. and his stand for social justice and the role that the Constitution played.

What is Manu's role now?

Manusmirti once had a significant influence on society, particularly caste, gender, and social hierarchy. Now it is no longer followed by most people in India. The now India has a significant influence on constitutional values. The social reformers like dr have direct relevance in everyday life. The symbolic burning of the *Manusmriti* by Dr. Ambedkar was not merely a rejection of an ancient text but a broader condemnation of the discriminatory ideologies that survived through generations. Even as India moves forward, embracing constitutional rights and democratic values, the echoes of such ancient codes remind us why continuous social reform and critical reflection are necessary.

Recognizing that *Manusmriti* is no longer followed by most does not negate its historical significance or its lingering effects. It compels us to reflect on how far we have come—and how much further we need to go to achieve true social justice.

Gender inequality

This is not just in India this is a global issue. gender-based inequality in schools, in college, at home, at work every everywhere we face gender inequality. This is one of the most rooted forms of injustice across cultures, religions, and historical periods. Even in this 21st century we still face these inequalities but the only thing that keeps us remained of how far we have come from where it all started the journey from being confined within the four walls of our homes to claiming spaces in schools, workplaces, and leadership positions is a testament to the resilience and determination of countless women and gender-rights advocates across generations. Equality is a never-ending social fabric. even today women are less represented in boardrooms and politics where Prower plays a major role. The irony lies in the fact that while laws may proclaim equality, lived realities often tell a different story. However, acknowledging this paradox is the first step towards change. It seeks to question, to understand, and most importantly, to inspire action. Because true equality is not just about what we've achieved but about what we're still fighting for. We need a whole new book to discuss about this hope fully my next book will be on gender inequality. At its core, gender inequality refers to the unequal treatment or perception of individuals based on their gender. This inequality manifests in various forms—social, economic, political, legal, and cultural—affecting access to resources, opportunities, and rights. While women experience discrimination other genders still have not even been started to recognize such as transgender, non-binary, and intersex individuals face layers of marginalization that are mostly unknown, unnoticed, and outright ignored. The roots of gender inequality are embedded again in the ancient texts prescribing a woman's role as subordinate to men both in the family and society. The narrative of male dominance and female subservience was passed down through generations, normalizing the suppression of women's rights to education, property, political participation, and bodily autonomy.

Yet, The evolution from domestic confines to influential roles in education, careers, and leadership highlights the relentless spirit and perseverance of women and gender equality champions throughout history. The struggle against gender inequality is not just about breaking physical barriers but dismantling the invisible chains of societal expectations, stereotypes, and systemic biases. **"Freedom, especially freedom for women, is not something that needs to be given; it is their own inherent right, not**

a privilege to be granted but a birthright to be lived, claimed, and celebrated."

As we unravel into Insights India and Its Complex Social Fabric it becomes evident that our society is a tapestry woven with threads of tradition, diversity, conflict, and change. Each strand tells a story—of caste and class, of gender and identity, of privilege and oppression. These narratives are not just relics of the past but living realities that continue to influence the present and shape the future. Understanding this intricate weave is essential, not just to comprehend India's historical journey, but to recognize the resilience, struggles, and aspirations of those who have fought—and continue to fight—for a more just and equal society. It is within this complexity that the true spirit of India resides, both fragile and fierce, ever-evolving yet deeply rooted."

"Past discrimination based on birth should never define us. Though progress has been made, the fight for equality continues."

THE PAST AND PRESENT OF CASTE AND INDIA

> *"Caste is not a physical object like a wall of bricks or a line of barbed wire which prevents the Hindus from coalescing, but it is a notion, it is a state of the mind"*
>
> **– Dr. BR. Ambedkar**

India is a land of immense diversity, but caste is not a reflection of that diversity—it is a form of discrimination. For centuries, caste has been deeply embedded in our society, and despite progress, it continues to persist. India is rich in its social structure, yet caste remains a defining factor in social interactions, opportunities, and identities. From the unimaginable torture of caste in the past to a far better present, India's journey has been one of struggle and resistance. While progress has been made, the shadows of caste discrimination still linger, reminding us that the fight for true equality is far from over.

The rigid adherence to the caste system has historically led to the dominance of upper-caste groups over lower-caste communities. The plebeians were treated as if they were insignificant, denied basic rights, and subjected to inhumane discrimination. Untouchability, a cruel practice, forced Dalits to live on the fringes of villages, prohibited them from drawing water from common wells, and barred them from entering temples. They were assigned degrading jobs such as manual scavenging, which further reinforced social hierarchies. Even in education, lower-caste individuals were denied access to schools, limiting their opportunities for progress."**The dominators imposed harsh restrictions on Dalits, especially in the realm of education, deliberately denying them the opportunity to rise and thrive."**

Leaders like Dr. B.R. Ambedkar, Jyotirao Phule, and Periyar fought against this systemic oppression, demanding equality and justice. Though legal reforms like the abolition of untouchability under Article 17 of the Indian Constitution have brought change, caste discrimination still manifests in various forms today. India's past has never been a period of great progress for many, especially for those belonging to the lower castes. If we look at the numbers, lower-caste communities have always been the majority, yet they have historically faced systemic oppression and exclusion. Despite their large numbers, they were denied access to education, economic opportunities, and social mobility, ensuring that power remained concentrated in the hands of the upper castes.

The Shudras

The Shudras are the lowest of all, The Shudras have historically been positioned at the lowest rung of the Varna system. Dr. B.R. Ambedkar, in *Who Were the Shudras?*, raises fundamental questions about the origins of the Shudras and their place in the Varna system. Contrary to the conventional belief that the Shudras were inherently a servile class, Ambedkar argues that they were originally part of the Kshatriya (warrior) community. However, due to historical conflicts and social exclusion, they were later relegated to the lowest position in the Varna hierarchy.

One of the key texts Ambedkar examines is the *Purusha Sukta* of the *Rig Veda*, which describes the Shudras as originating from the feet of the cosmic being, Purusha. This classification placed them at the lowest tier of the Varna system, denying them rights and privileges granted to the other three Varnas—Brahmins, Kshatriyas, and Vaishyas. Ambedkar critiques this as a constructed hierarchy meant to justify the subjugation of a particular group rather than a natural order of society. He further explains that lately sudras were denied t access to education, religious scriptures, and to enter temples.

The Flawed Logic of Birth-based Hierarchies

If all of this is based on a division and discrimination determined by only birth, what is the point of it? How can anyone claim to be superior or inferior simply because they were born into a particular family? One person does what is considered "pure" work, and another does what is deemed "impure," all just because of the family they were born into.

The assumption that a person is inherently "upper" or "lower" based on their birth in a particular caste fails to account for the diverse potential of individuals. Birth, which is beyond anyone's control, should not be a determinant of worth or ability. If a person is born into a "higher" caste, it doesn't mean they are inherently more capable or virtuous. Likewise, if someone is born into a "lower" caste, it doesn't make their work or contributions inherently inferior.

This framework of discrimination based on birth leads to a skewed understanding of human dignity, which, in reality, should be founded on an individual's actions, character, and contributions to society—not on an arbitrary factor like their family or caste.

The Rule of upper caste and lower caste

The concept of caste in Indian culture has been historically significant in shaping social, economic, and political dynamics. The distinction between the upper and lower castes has influenced society for many years. Upper castes traditionally held positions of power and privilege while downcastes faced systemic discrimination and marginalization This socio-political divide known under the name of the "caste hierarchy" has resulted in disparities in access to resources opportunities and justice. Over the years numerous social movements and constitutional provisions have aimed at addressing caste-based inequalities. However, the rule of upper caste dominance and the plight of lower castes remain central problems in contemporary Indian society. The hierarchy that places the upper castes at the top of the social pyramid and the lower castes at the bottom stems from the historical context of the Varna system. This structure allowed the upper castes to consolidate power, wealth, and privilege, while systematically suppressing the lower castes.

The Practices of Untouchability

As I mentioned earlier, India's history was far from pleasant, particularly for Dalits, who were treated as being lower than animals.For centuries, India has carried the weight of caste on its shoulders. As Dr. rightly pointed out in his book *The Untouchables*, Dalits were forced to live on the outskirts of villages, away from the so-called "pure" castes. They were denied access to common resources such as wells and temples and were even prohibited from walking on the same streets as upper castes. Their very existence was deemed polluting, making them outcasts in their own land.

At this point, I am reminded of something deeply significant—India is home to some of the world's most extraordinary architectural wonders, particularly its temples. These grand structures are not just places of worship but living chronicles of our civilization, with their walls etched with history and their foundations rooted in centuries of tradition. They have endured time, conquests, and revolutions, standing as symbols of our collective heritage. Yet, the greatest irony is that while these temples were built to honor divinity, they have long been used to uphold human-made divisions. The very spaces meant to unite people in faith became tools of exclusion, barring entry to those deemed "impure" by an unjust social order. No temple, no place of worship, belongs to a select few. They belong to the people—the entire people—without exception. To deny entry based on caste is not just a denial of faith but a betrayal of the very essence of spirituality itself. "True devotion cannot coexist with discrimination, and no tradition can justify the injustice of exclusion". "True devotion cannot coexist with discrimination, and no tradition can justify the injustice of exclusion."

When every god in this world teaches us that all are equal, how can we reconcile the idea that some are superior and others inferior based solely on birth? If the divine is about unity and equality, how can we allow the belief that one person is born 'higher' than another to dictate who can enter sacred spaces? It's a contradiction at its core—how can there be true spirituality when some believe they are superior and others are relegated to the position of 'the other' simply because of their caste? There cannot be spiritual peace when division is so deeply ingrained in the very fabric of faith.

And so, if you truly believe in God, remember that you don't need to step into a temple to find divinity. God is everywhere—in every moment, in every action, in every heart. The idea that God is confined to one space is a human-made restriction. True faith transcends boundaries; it's not about where you pray but how you live and treat others with equality and respect.

And if you don't believe, then that is simply better. For true spirituality has no need for exclusion, for it exists in the belief that all are equal—without the need for any divisions, spaces, or barriers.

I can't miss *Joothan*—a book that made me truly realize and deeply understand the past life of Dalits, not in some distant history, but in a past that still lingers, a past that breathes within the present. Om Prakash Valmiki's words hit hard, not just as a personal narrative but as a testimony of pain, humiliation, and injustice that Dalits had to endure every single day. Being forced to sit separately in school, beaten for daring to dream, and pushed into degrading work simply because of birth—his life wasn't just his own, but a reflection of millions. *Joothan* opened my eyes to the weight of untouchability, a burden carried not by choice but by force. It made me see how caste was not just about exclusion—it was about stripping away dignity, leaving behind nothing but suffering and silence.

When I read this book, I couldn't help but whisper a quiet *thank you*—to every single person who fought for change. It may not be a complete transformation, it may not be a world where discrimination has vanished entirely, but it is a world far better than the past. The struggles, the voices, the sacrifices—they did not go in vain. We still have a long way to go, but at least today, we can speak, we can question, we can demand what was once denied. And for that, I am grateful.

Untouchability was not just about physical exclusion; it was an intricate web of oppression that seeped into every aspect of daily life, ensuring that Dalits remained at the absolute bottom of society. They were denied the right to wear decent clothing or even footwear in the presence of upper castes, a deliberate act to mark their subjugation. Forced into the most degrading and inhumane jobs, Dalits were made to clean human waste, remove dead animals, and perform other tasks designed to rob them of dignity.

Their economic exploitation was just as brutal. Dalits were forced to labor for upper-caste landlords, often receiving leftover food instead of wages. And when they were paid, it was barely enough to survive, keeping them in an unbreakable cycle of poverty. This system wasn't just about keeping Dalits poor—it was about ensuring they remained dependent on their oppressors, never allowed the means to break free, and never given the chance to dream of a life beyond suffering.

The upper castes knew exactly what they were doing—building a system so rigid and oppressive that those at the bottom could never rise. They didn't just discriminate; they ensured that the so-called lower castes remained trapped in a never-ending cycle of oppression, poverty, and indignity. But let's not sugarcoat it—the caste system is nothing but an engineered lie, a brutal hierarchy designed to benefit the privileged at the cost of millions. It is the most absurd and cruel invention, deciding a person's worth not by their abilities, character, or choices, but by something as arbitrary as birth.

Untouchability was never just about keeping Dalits physically separate; it was about crushing them mentally, emotionally, and economically, making sure they remained at the bottom with no way to rise. The caste system was built on a carefully designed cruelty that ensured lower castes remained dependent on those above them, with no path to dignity or financial independence. History has witnessed horrific incidents where Dalits paid the price for daring to challenge this oppressive order.

The **Kilvenmani Massacre (1968, Tamil Nadu)** stands as one of the most brutal examples of how caste oppression was enforced with blood. Dalit agricultural workers had the audacity to demand better wages and working conditions, something that should have been their basic right. But instead of justice, they were met with fire. A mob of upper-caste landlords set a hut ablaze while Dalit women, children, and men were trapped inside, burning **44 innocent people alive**. Their only crime? Asking for what was rightfully theirs.

Decades later, caste violence remained as monstrous as ever. The **Kherlanji Massacre (2006, Maharashtra)** was not just a murder; it was an act of calculated, merciless cruelty meant to instill fear. A Dalit family that refused to bow down to upper-caste dominance was **publicly stripped, paraded naked, beaten, raped, and murdered**. The police, the system, and even society itself turned a blind eye, proving that caste atrocities are not just acts of individuals but the result of deep-seated structural oppression.

And it never stopped. The **Bhagana Case (2014, Haryana)** showed how Dalit women are the easiest targets of caste brutality. Four young Dalit girls were abducted and sexually assaulted, their dignity ripped away simply because their families had dared to stand against their eviction from the village. Even after protests, justice was slow, and the silence of the authorities was deafening.

The **Una Flogging Incident (2016, Gujarat)** proved how caste-based violence is disguised under new justifications. Dalit men were doing what they had been forced to do for generations—skinning a dead cow—when they were **brutally beaten with iron rods, stripped, and humiliated in public** by self-proclaimed "protectors of culture." The video of the attack sparked outrage, but the reality is that such humiliation has been a daily reality for Dalits for centuries.

Caste discrimination starts early, targeting even the youngest. Schools, meant to be places of learning, become breeding grounds for untouchability. Dalit children are **made to sit separately, not allowed to drink from the same water pots, and even punished for daring to exist in these spaces.** In **2019, in Uttar Pradesh**, a young Dalit boy named Raja Jaipal Singh was **beaten to death by his teacher**—his only crime? Drinking water from a pot meant for upper-caste students. What kind of society decides a child's right to drink water based on his birth?

These are not stories of the distant past. This is not ancient history. This is India's reality—one that many refuse to acknowledge, one that millions are forced to endure every single day. The system has ensured that even after decades of struggle, justice is still a luxury Dalits cannot afford. The question is, **how much longer will we allow this to continue?**

Who gave anyone the right to decide that one human is superior while another is destined to live in chains, simply because of their caste? No one is born lesser. No tradition, no belief system, and no outdated ideology should ever have the power to strip someone of their rights, dignity, or humanity. Every single person is born with potential, dreams, and the right to shape their own life. It is not caste but courage, not birth but brilliance, and not privilege but perseverance that should determine a person's place in this world. Anyone who believes otherwise is clinging to a past built on oppression—and that past has no place in the present or the future.

We have come a long way—from being brutally tortured for simply existing to at least having a space to live, from being denied wages to owning businesses, from having caste labels forced upon us to proudly holding just our own names. But let's not mistake progress for completion. The journey is far from over. The battle is not just about where we have reached but about how far we still need to go. And we will go that distance—because if history has taught us anything, it is that **consistency is our greatest weapon.**

To those who wonder, *"Does caste still exist?"* or even question, *"Is caste-based discrimination still a thing?"*—the answer is simple. If you have never encountered caste, it only means that **you have never had to face its brutality.** It means you have never been told where to sit, what to eat, or how to live based on your birth. And that, in itself, is a privilege carved out of **centuries of resistance, pain, and struggle by those who refused to accept oppression as fate.**

If you have never felt the weight of caste, be grateful—but do not assume it has disappeared. It only means that someone, somewhere, fought long and hard enough to ensure that you wouldn't have to bear it. And that fight is not over yet.

An Ongoing Struggle for Equality

"Caste is not just a relic of the past; it is a living force, influencing our choices, relationships, and aspirations, even in the 21st century."

While India has made significant strides in many areas—economic growth, technological progress, and global recognition—caste remains a pervasive influence on the lives of millions. The deep-rooted inequalities linked to caste continue to shape society, often in ways that are invisible yet powerful. From access to education and employment to social interactions and legal justice, caste continues to inform how individuals experience their world, creating barriers that many are still unable to overcome.

In this section, we will examine the present-day reality of caste in India—how it continues to impact social mobility, economic opportunities, and legal protections. Despite ongoing efforts to address these issues, caste remains a formidable force that challenges the idea of true equality. This struggle, however, is not without hope, as continued social reforms and legal changes attempt to break down these barriers, though much more remains to be done.

Despite the progress India has made in the modern era, caste continues to cast a long shadow over its society, leaving deep scars that are hard to heal. Caste-based discrimination in employment remains rampant, with lower-caste individuals still relegated to menial jobs, regardless of their qualifications or skills. In educational institutions, Dalit students face subtle yet pervasive forms of bullying and exclusion, hindering their chances of succeeding in a system that was supposed to be built on merit. The choice to marry outside one's caste—while seen as a personal freedom—often invites violent opposition, leading to tragic consequences such as honor killings, exposing the brutality of caste's grip on personal lives. Caste-based violence, though condemned by the law, continues to occur with alarming regularity, particularly in rural areas, where Dalits are still subjected to physical assault and even murder for defying caste norms. Social segregation, though less visible in urban spaces, still thrives in the form of caste-based colonies, where communities are divided by invisible yet unbreakable lines. Even the reservation system, meant to uplift the marginalized, has become a flashpoint for divisive debates, often exacerbating the divide it was designed to heal. These stark realities reveal an undeniable truth: caste is not merely a historical relic; it is an ongoing force, shaping lives, identities, and destinies, and its impact is far from over.

The 2020 Hathras gang rape and murder shook me to my core. A young Dalit woman, brutally assaulted and left to die by upper-caste men, was denied justice not only by the perpetrators but also by a system that failed to protect her. The shocking haste with which her body was cremated by authorities, without her family's consent, revealed the harsh reality of caste-based oppression that still permeates every corner of our society. It stoked my heart with anger and sorrow, reminding me that caste, even today, continues to determine the fate of millions. This was not just a crime against a woman; it was a crime against humanity, exposing the callous disregard for Dalit lives. Similarly, the Palghar lynching in Maharashtra, where two priests from a lower caste were killed by a mob, underscored how caste prejudice continues to ignite violence. These incidents are not isolated—they reflect a harsh truth: caste, in its many forms, is still a powerful force that dictates who gets to live with dignity and who does not.

In a disturbing incident that occurred in the Indian Parliament, a member from the ruling party questioned the Leader of Opposition

(LOP) by saying, "You don't even know what your caste is; you should feel ashamed of it." This statement not only shocked me but also saddened me deeply, as such words came from the very institution meant to uphold democracy and equality. What compounded my dismay was when the Prime Minister posted this speech on social media, encouraging others to adopt this stance and make it the norm. In a country like India, where we have enshrined laws in our Constitution to protect citizens from discrimination, such an incident made me a question: Is our democracy truly fulfilling its role if this kind of caste-based intolerance is allowed to thrive? It felt like a blow to the ideals that our nation's democratic process should stand for. The ease with which casteist remarks were made and the public endorsement of such views left me wondering if our country's commitment to equality and justice had eroded over time.

However, amidst this disheartening incident, there was a moment of hope. The LOP responded with grace and dignity, saying, "Yes, I don't know my caste, and I am not ashamed of it." This response struck a chord with me. It was a powerful affirmation of the stand we should all take when confronted with caste-based humiliation: to reject it outright, to stand firm in our dignity, and to never let anyone diminish us based on the social labels that divide us. His words reminded me that true strength lies not in conforming to these divisive ideas, but in standing unapologetically for equality and humanity. This is the mindset we must adopt to dismantle the oppressive structures that still prevail in our society today.

In conclusion, the persistence of caste in India is a painful truth we cannot ignore. Despite the legal safeguards and promises of equality in our Constitution, the stark reality is that caste still defines too many lives, determines opportunities, and shapes destinies. As I reflect on incidents like the Hathras tragedy and the disturbing words spoken in Parliament, I can't help but question how far we've truly come. How is it possible for such blatant caste-based hatred to persist in a nation that claims to be democratic, just, and equal? It makes me wonder if our democracy is failing when casteism continues to thrive in places that should stand for progress.

But despite this darkness, I refuse to lose hope. The strength, courage, and dignity shown by those who rise above casteism—like the Leader of the Opposition—remind me that change is possible. His simple yet profound response, standing tall in the face of hate, is the attitude we all need to adopt. It's this kind of courage that can slowly but surely chip away at the deep-rooted structures of inequality. My vision for India is one where caste no longer has a hold over us, where we see each other as equals and stand united in our humanity. The road is long, but I believe that together, with conviction and a collective will, we can create a future where the true essence of equality isn't just a concept but a lived reality for all. This is a fight I believe in, and one I will continue to be a part of, no matter how challenging it may seem.

INDIAN CONSTITUTION AND CASTE

"We are going to enter a life. Of contradictions. In Politics, we will have equality, and in social & economic life, we will have inequality"

– Dr. BR.Ambedkar

When it comes to this topic, I am reminded of Dr. B.R. Ambedkar's powerful words: *"Equality is the soul of the Constitution."* Dr. Ambedkar, the man behind India's Constitution, is often called the "Father of the Indian Constitution." India's Constitution, the world's largest written constitution, stands as a testament to the vision of a just and equal society, a society where every individual, regardless of their background, could claim their rightful place.

For centuries, the caste system in India was not merely a social hierarchy but a rigid framework that determined one's access to education, opportunities, and dignity. It permeated every aspect of life, relegating millions to lives of discrimination and deprivation. Dr. Ambedkar, himself a victim of caste-based discrimination, understood the weight of this oppression. When the time came to frame a new legal framework for independent India, he did not just see it as a task of drafting laws; he saw it as an opportunity to challenge and dismantle the social order that had kept millions suppressed for generations. Through his tireless efforts, he ensured that the Constitution would protect the rights of the marginalized and guarantee equality for all citizens.

This chapter delves into the Constitution's provisions designed to combat caste-based discrimination and promote social justice, highlighting the critical role of legal protection in the journey toward an egalitarian society.

The Constitution's Preamble and Equality

The **Preamble** of the Indian Constitution serves as the cornerstone of the nation's legal and political framework. It eloquently embodies the core values and aspirations envisioned by its framers, reflecting the ideals upon which independent India was built. Every word in the Preamble guarantees **equality**, reinforcing India's commitment to **justice**, **liberty**, and **fraternity**. The Preamble goes beyond mere words; it encapsulates the grand vision of an inclusive and democratic India, where governance is centered on the people, and equality is ensured across all sectors of society. The essence of the Preamble lies in its emphasis on **fairness** and **unity**, aiming to unite a diverse population under a common constitutional framework. Though not legally enforceable, the Preamble remains a guiding principle, often referenced in judicial interpretations to understand the underlying intent and spirit of the Constitution's provisions. Courts have consistently turned to the Preamble to shed light on ambiguous or unclear sections, making it a cornerstone in constitutional interpretation.

The opening words, *"We, the People of India,"* carry profound significance. They affirm that sovereignty lies with the people, signifying a rejection of foreign domination and monarchical rule. This powerful phrase establishes India as a **democratic** republic, where the ultimate power resides with its citizens. It highlights that governance is not dictated by a ruler but by the collective will of the people, ensuring that every citizen, irrespective of **caste**, **creed**, or **class**, plays an equal role in the shaping of the nation. The Preamble also lays down five key political principles—**sovereignty**, **socialism**, **secularism**, **democracy**, and **republicanism**—which guide the country's governance, lawmaking, and public policies.

Sovereignty ensures that India exercises full control over its internal and external affairs, formulating policies independently and free from external influence. It is central to India's national identity and autonomy. **Socialism** envisions a society where economic justice is a primary objective, focusing on reducing inequalities, ensuring equitable distribution of resources, and balancing the roles of both the **public** and **private sectors** in the economy. The inclusion of **secularism** in the Preamble highlights the commitment to religious harmony, ensuring that the state remains neutral in religious matters and that all faiths are treated with equal respect and dignity. **Democracy** guarantees political power vested in the people, ensuring that governance is carried out through **free and fair elections**. The Preamble's reference to **republicanism** ensures that leadership in India is based on merit and chosen by the people through elections, rather than inherited through dynastic rule. This principle promotes accountability and democratic participation, ensuring that political power remains in the hands of the people.

Despite these noble principles, India's political landscape today faces numerous challenges that test the resilience of these ideals. **External influences**, both geopolitical and economic, at times overshadow India's sovereign decision-making, leading to tensions in formulating independent policies. Internal conflicts, such as communal strife and growing political polarization, pose challenges to the **secular** fabric of the nation. Economic disparities continue to widen, with growing gaps between the rich and the poor, undermining the **socialist** vision of equitable development. The **democratic** spirit of the country is often tested by concerns about the integrity of the electoral process, the role of money in politics, and the concentration of power in the hands of a few. The rise of **dynastic politics** has also raised questions about the true realization of **republicanism**, as political leadership in some instances is still dictated by family legacies rather than merit or popular choice.

Although the Preamble continues to be the guiding light of India's Constitution, its values face ongoing scrutiny in today's political climate. The ideal of an inclusive, equal, and just society requires constant reaffirmation. To ensure that India remains faithful to its foundational principles, it is essential to address these challenges and work towards revitalizing the vision laid out in the Preamble. Strengthening constitutional values and bridging the gaps between idealism and political realities will safeguard the commitment to justice, equality, and unity, ensuring that India's democracy remains true to its original vision.

Key Provisions in the Constitution Addressing Caste Discrimination

The Constitution of India is not just a legal document.
It is the soul of a nation determined to rise — a nation that chose democracy over division, justice over centuries of injustice.

When India became free, it didn't simply shed foreign rule. It declared war against every form of inequality, especially the deeply rooted curse of caste. The Constitution stands as a testament to that battle, carving out a path toward dignity, fairness, and true equality for every citizen.

Have you ever looked at your passport carefully?
It doesn't just say "India."
It says "Republic of India."

That single word — **Republic** — carries the weight of our dreams.
It means we are not ruled by kings or by inherited privilege.
It means no one is born to govern, and no one is born to serve.
It means that leadership, rights, and dignity come from merit and collective will — not from caste, lineage, or history.

The Republic demands that equality is not just a promise — it must be a practice.
And that's why the Constitution strikes directly at caste discrimination, refusing to allow the injustices of the past to shape the future.

At the heart of this constitutional revolution are powerful weapons:

- **Article 14**: It smashes arbitrary discrimination, guaranteeing equality before the law and equal protection under it — regardless of caste.
- **Article 15**: It boldly prohibits discrimination based on religion, race, caste, sex, or place of birth — ensuring that public spaces and services belong to all.
- **Article 16**: It extends the fight into public employment, promising equal opportunity while empowering the State to take affirmative action for those historically crushed by injustice.
- **Article 17**: It does not stop at words. It abolishes untouchability, criminalizes its practice, and sends a message: caste oppression has no place in free India.

These articles are not just clauses.
They are India's constitutional commitment to tear down centuries of injustice.

But the fight doesn't end there.

Other key provisions strengthen the shield:

- **Article 46**: Orders the State to promote the educational and economic interests of SCs, STs, and OBCs.
- **Article 15(4)**: Empowers special measures, like reservations, to uplift historically oppressed communities.
- **Article 29**: Protects the cultural and educational rights of minorities, ensuring no community is erased or excluded.

- **Article 335**: Balances justice with administrative efficiency, making sure the claims of SCs and STs are respected in public employment.
- **Article 340**: Creates commissions to study the conditions of backward classes and recommend real measures for their advancement.

Together, these provisions do more than promise change. They demand it.

They remind us that democracy without social justice is hollow — and that the Republic of India must belong equally to every citizen, not just in law, but in life.

The Role of Affirmative Action

Affirmative action in India is not about giving someone an unfair advantage. It is about breaking the chains of centuries-old inequality, where millions were denied the very basics—education, dignity, opportunity—because of the caste they were born into. These constitutional safeguards are not just policy tools; they are moral correctives. They are India's promise to itself—that it will not repeat the injustice of its past.

The Indian Constitution enshrines the idea that those who were historically excluded must now be included. Scheduled Castes (SCs), Scheduled Tribes (STs), and Other Backward Classes (OBCs) receive support through reservations in education, employment, and political representation—not as a favor, but as a right. These measures aim to level a field that was once steeply tilted.

Reservations are one part of a broader vision. Scholarships, coaching support, and financial aid programs help bridge gaps in access to quality education. Skill development schemes and entrepreneurship drives are building pathways to economic independence. It's not about charity. It's about justice.

Yet, affirmative action has drawn criticism. Some say caste-based reservations should be replaced with economic criteria. Others argue that such policies should be phased out. But these critiques often ignore a crucial truth: caste discrimination is still alive—silent, subtle, and systemic.

Let's address a common myth—that one community takes everything. Here's the truth:

15% is reserved for Scheduled Castes.

7.5% for Scheduled Tribes.

27% for OBCs.

10% for the Economically Weaker Sections (EWS).

These figures aren't arbitrary—they reflect population realities and historical marginalization. The remaining seats go to unreserved categories. No one is being denied opportunity; instead, opportunities are being rebalanced.

Some students from OBC or BC backgrounds express frustration, thinking that only SCs benefit. But when you step back and look at the whole picture—the numbers, the population share, the allocation—you see fairness, not favoritism.

Let's Talk Merit

People who scream "merit!" must first answer—how do you define merit in a country where children grow up with different levels of safety, sanitation, schooling, and social stigma?

When the starting line is tilted, cheering for the fastest runner isn't merit—it's privilege in disguise.

The Race of Opportunity

Let's take a different lens—a story. Let's title it The Race of Opportunity.

Imagine four students at the starting line of a race that will decide their future.

Rahul comes from an affluent family. Private schooling, top tutors, and every learning resource—he has it all.

Meena is from a modest background. She studies in a government school with limited resources but is determined and hardworking.

Arjun lives in a remote village. His school lacks teachers, and he helps on the farm after class. He studies under a flickering lightbulb.

Priya is from a marginalized caste. Her family has never seen formal education. She's the first to even dream of a different life. She fights prejudice daily—at school, in society, even in her own home.

Now imagine the starting line.

Rahul stands 50 meters ahead. Meena is 20 meters forward. Arjun and Priya are placed far behind—even before the race begins.

The whistle blows. They all run.

Can we call this a fair race?

Affirmative action is not about pulling someone ahead unfairly. It's about bringing Arjun and Priya to the starting line—not to give them a win, but to finally let them run on equal ground.

India's goal is not to reserve forever. The ultimate aim is that one day, reservation won't be needed—because caste would no longer define destiny. But until that day comes, affirmative action remains the bridge between the unequal past and the just future.

The Challenge of Implementation

Many who haven't personally faced caste discrimination or seen its impact firsthand might believe it's a thing of the past. With multiple constitutional provisions against caste-based discrimination, some argue that the issue should no longer persist. But the real challenge isn't just having laws on paper—it's ensuring they are effectively put into action. Ensuring that these laws are followed is no easy task. Loopholes in the legal system create a stark contrast between what the law states and what actually happens on the ground. Fixing this requires more than just legal frameworks; it demands strict enforcement and a collective commitment from society to uphold true equality. The failure of law enforcement is not just evident in cases of caste-based violence but also in the everyday lives of those trapped in systemic discrimination. Despite being outlawed under the Prohibition of Employment as Manual Scavengers and Their Rehabilitation Act, 2013, manual scavenging persists in many regions. This practice, deeply rooted in caste oppression, highlights how legal bans mean little when alternative livelihoods and rehabilitation measures are not effectively provided. It reflects a larger pattern of neglect—one where laws exist, but the will to implement them remains weak, keeping marginalized communities bound to their historical oppression. Even when legal protections exist, they are not immune to dilution. In 2018, the Supreme Court weakened key provisions of the Scheduled Castes and Scheduled Tribes (Prevention of Atrocities) Act by introducing safeguards against alleged misuse. This sparked widespread protests, compelling the government to reverse the dilution and restore the act's original intent. The episode underscored how judicial interpretations can sometimes erode protective laws, forcing marginalized communities into an exhausting cycle of advocacy and resistance just to retain their basic rights. It was yet another indication that legal battles do not end with the passing of a law; rather, they require constant vigilance to prevent regression. These real-world cases expose the harsh truth: having laws is not enough.

The persistence of manual scavenging revealed the hollowness of laws that are not enforced on the ground. The dilution of the SC/ST Act demonstrated how protective legislation itself can be weakened under the guise of reform. Without stringent enforcement, systemic accountability, and a collective societal will to uphold justice, caste-based discrimination continues to thrive, making equality a distant reality. These cases serve as a call to action—demanding not just legal solutions, but a fundamental shift in how we implement and uphold the promise of justice.

Role of Institutions in Combating Caste-Based Discrimination

Institutions play a decisive role in either dismantling or perpetuating caste-based discrimination, shaping the lived realities of millions in India. The legal system, despite its strong constitutional safeguards against caste oppression, often falls short in enforcement. While laws like the SC/ST (Prevention of Atrocities) Act exist, justice remains elusive for many victims due to delayed trials, police inaction, and societal pressure to withdraw complaints. The 2016 Una incident, where Dalit men were brutally assaulted for skinning a dead cow, exemplifies this failure—despite laws against such violence, it was the collective outrage and protests that forced authorities to act. Similarly, educational institutions, which should serve as spaces of empowerment, often become arenas of exclusion. The suicide of Rohith Vemula, a Dalit PhD scholar at the University of Hyderabad, highlighted how systemic biases push marginalized students to the brink. Casteist slurs, academic gatekeeping, and lack of institutional support continue to make higher education a struggle for many Dalit and Adivasi students. Political institutions, too, reflect this deep-rooted discrimination. While caste-based vote banks remain a defining feature of Indian elections, genuine representation of marginalized communities in positions of power remains minimal. The reality that manual scavenging still exists despite its legal ban under the

2013 Act speaks volumes about the failure of governance in ensuring real change. Social and cultural institutions, particularly religious spaces, have long been complicit in reinforcing caste hierarchies, with temple entry restrictions and segregated seating in rituals persisting even today. However, social movements and media have emerged as powerful forces of resistance, amplifying the voices of the oppressed. The Bhim Army's fight for Dalit rights and the growing presence of Dalit-led media platforms are reshaping narratives once controlled by upper-caste gatekeepers. Even corporate institutions are not immune to caste-based biases, as seen in hiring practices where certain surnames still dictate access to opportunities. Despite a few progressive initiatives like diversity hiring programs in major firms, caste-based wage gaps and discrimination remain unaddressed in many sectors. At the heart of all these institutions are people—families and communities that uphold or challenge these hierarchies. The way children are raised, the biases ingrained within families, and the social norms enforced in everyday life collectively sustain or dismantle caste oppression. True change requires not just legal reforms but a fundamental shift in societal mindset, where institutions don't just function on paper but actively work towards an equitable reality. Only then can India move beyond tokenistic measures and towards real justice.

Let me tell you, grassroots activism and public awareness are absolutely crucial when it comes to enforcing laws. Look at movements like **#MeToo** or the protests after the **Nirbhaya case** – these weren't just people raising their voices; they were demanding action, making sure that the laws are not just words on paper but something that impacts real lives. It's clear that public participation drives the justice system, but here's the problem: despite all these efforts, the real challenge comes in the form of systemic barriers. **Corruption**, political interference, and a lack of resources constantly hold us back.

Take the Vyapam scam in Madhya Pradesh, where large-scale manipulation of entrance exams in education and government jobs revealed how corruption undermines meritocracy. For Dalits and Adivasis who already face systemic barriers, such scams further limit access to upward mobility, making the promise of reservation and representation meaningless in practice.

And Take the case of sanitation workers—many of whom come from Dalit communities—who are still made to clean sewers manually despite mechanization policies. Their deaths, often due to toxic gases, reflect not just institutional apathy but deep-rooted caste prejudice masquerading as neglect.

Now, what do we do about it? First, we need **legal reforms**, but let me be clear – when we talk about reforming laws, it shouldn't mean overriding the original framework of the Constitution. The Constitution is the foundation, and any reforms should only serve to **extend** the law or add provisions to meet current needs. It should never replace or dilute the core values enshrined in the original document. Think of it like adding new chapters to an existing book – the essence of the book stays intact, but we add content to address the evolving world. Legal reforms must **complement** the Constitution, not contradict it.. Imagine a system where we can **track cases digitally** – we've seen glimpses of this with the **e-courts project**, but it needs to be expanded. Digital tracking can speed up cases and make the process more transparent. And don't forget about **stricter penalties**. When people know the consequences for their actions are severe – like in the **Satyam scandal** – it forces them to think twice before breaking the law. Finally, we need to keep educating the public. If people know their rights and understand how the law works, they're more likely to demand justice and hold those in power accountable. We need a shift in how we think about law and order – not just in theory, but in practice. If we make these changes, we'll start seeing a real difference in how laws are applied, and more importantly, how they impact our lives

Judicial Interpretation of Constitutional Provisions

Judicial interpretation of constitutional provisions is what keeps a democracy alive and evolving. Think of the Indian judiciary as the guardian of the Constitution—its role isn't just about enforcing laws but also about shaping their meaning to fit a changing society. The Indian Constitution is vast, and its provisions are sometimes open to multiple interpretations. That's where the courts step in, bridging the gap between legal texts and real-world governance. Every major judgment has implications that touch our daily lives—be it individual rights, social justice, or the power dynamics between the branches of government.

The Basic Structure Doctrine

Let's start with a game-changer in constitutional law—the **Basic Structure Doctrine**. It all began with the landmark case of *Kesavananda Bharati v. State of Kerala (1973)*. The Supreme Court ruled that while Parliament can amend the Constitution, it cannot change its fundamental identity. This ensures that core principles—like democracy, secularism, and the rule of law—remain untouched, no matter who's in power. Think of it as a safety net that prevents reckless amendments. A perfect example? When the Supreme Court struck down the **NJAC Act (2015)** to protect judicial independence, reinforcing that the judiciary should remain free from political influence.

Modes of Constitutional Interpretation

How should courts interpret the Constitution? There are two broad approaches—**originalism** (sticking to the framers' intent) and **evolutionary interpretation** (adapting the Constitution to modern realities). India leans towards the latter, as seen in *Maneka Gandhi v. Union of India (1978)*, where **Article 21** was expanded to include the right to live with dignity. This method has profound real-world effects: in *Anuradha Bhasin v. Union of India (2020)*, the Supreme Court recognized **internet access as a fundamental right**, showing how constitutional interpretation evolves with the times.

The Role of Precedents

Every judgment builds on the past, following the principle of **stare decisis** (let the decision stand). But sometimes, courts recognize the need for change. Take *Golaknath v. State of Punjab (1967)*—it declared that Parliament couldn't amend Fundamental Rights. Then, in *Kesavananda Bharati*, the Court modified this stance, allowing amendments but preserving the Constitution's basic structure. This ability to adapt is crucial. For example, in *Navtej Singh Johar v. Union of India (2018)*, the Court overruled a previous decision and decriminalized homosexuality, reflecting changing societal values.

The Preamble as a Guiding Light

The **Preamble** isn't just a decorative introduction—it's a guiding light for constitutional interpretation. Courts often turn to it when they need clarity on fundamental values like **justice, liberty, and equality**. In *Indira Sawhney v. Union of India (1992)*, the Supreme Court upheld reservations for backward classes as a step toward social justice, relying on the Preamble's principles. Similarly, in *Union of India v. R. Gandhi*

(2010), the Court used the Preamble to stress the importance of an independent judiciary.

Judicial Activism vs. Judicial Restraint

Sometimes, courts actively intervene to protect rights (**judicial activism**), while at other times, they step back to respect legislative decisions (**judicial restraint**). A bold example of activism is *K.S. Puttaswamy v. Union of India (2017)*, where the Supreme Court ruled that **Right to Privacy** is fundamental under **Article 21**. On the flip side, in *ADM Jabalpur v. Shivkant Shukla (1976)*, the Court upheld the suspension of fundamental rights during the Emergency—an example of excessive restraint, later criticized and overturned.

The Doctrine of Judicial Review

Judicial review is the power of courts to strike down unconstitutional laws and actions. It was first established in *Marbury v. Madison (1803)* in the U.S. and later became a cornerstone of Indian law. In *Minerva Mills Ltd. v. Union of India (1980)*, the Supreme Court reaffirmed that Fundamental Rights and Directive Principles must be harmonized. More recently, in *Shreya Singhal v. Union of India (2015)*, the Court struck down **Section 66A of the IT Act**, ensuring that free speech isn't stifled by vague laws.

Expansion of Fundamental Rights

One of the judiciary's most significant contributions has been the expansion of **Fundamental Rights**. In *Maneka Gandhi v. Union of India*, the Court transformed **Article 21** from a simple right to life into a broad protection of dignity. Fast forward to *Navtej Singh Johar v. Union of India (2018)*—the Court struck down **Section 377**, decriminalizing homosexuality. In *Joseph Shine v. Union of India (2018)*, adultery laws were scrapped, reinforcing personal liberty. These judgments prove that constitutional rights are meant to grow alongside society.

The Role of Directive Principles

Though **Directive Principles of State Policy (DPSPs)** aren't legally enforceable, they often shape judicial decisions. In *Minerva Mills*, the Supreme Court balanced DPSPs with Fundamental Rights, ensuring social welfare didn't override individual freedoms. A classic case is *M.C. Mehta v. Union of India*, where the Court invoked DPSPs to push for environmental protections. In *Mohini Jain v. State of Karnataka (1992)*, DPSPs played a key role in recognizing the **Right to Education**.

Public Interest Litigation (PIL) and Social Justice

Public Interest Litigation (PIL) has revolutionized access to justice in India. It allows individuals to file cases on behalf of those who can't afford legal representation. One of the most impactful cases, *Vishaka v. State of Rajasthan (1997)*, led to the creation of **guidelines for preventing sexual harassment at the workplace**, setting the stage for later legislation. PILs have played a crucial role in protecting bonded laborers, improving environmental policies, and holding law enforcement accountable.

Judicial interpretation isn't just about legal theories—it shapes the country we live in. Every landmark ruling affects governance, rights, and freedoms. Whether it's protecting democracy through the **Basic Structure Doctrine**, expanding **Fundamental Rights**, or addressing new-age issues like **privacy and internet freedom**, the judiciary ensures that the Constitution remains relevant. As society evolves, so must its laws, and judicial interpretation is the bridge that keeps them connected. The Constitution is not just a document; it's a living force, and the judiciary is its heartbeat.

The Reservation Debate: A Necessary Step or an Unfair Advantage?

Yes, we've already touched on reservation briefly, but let's dive deeper. It's a topic that sparks fierce debate, and for good reason. Some argue that it's an unfair advantage, while others defend it as the only way to correct centuries of oppression. But here's a thought: what if reservation isn't about giving some people a *head start*, but about *leveling the playing field* for all?

I want you to think about this: we live in a society where privilege isn't always obvious. It's not written on your face, but it's embedded in your education, your environment, your resources—and even your birth. Some of us are born into families where education isn't just a hope—it's a given. Others have to fight to even reach that starting line. So the real question is, do we pretend that everyone is on equal footing, or do we address this imbalance?

Let's break it down. Often, we hear that reservation disproportionately benefits a select few. But that's a narrow interpretation. Reservation is about *compensation*, not *privilege*. It's about giving those who have been historically oppressed a chance to catch up. Look at the OBCs, SCs, and STs—without reservation, how many of them would have access to quality education or jobs? The answer is far fewer than we care to admit.

We're talking about communities that have faced *systematic oppression* for centuries. That kind of inequality doesn't vanish overnight. So when people say, "Reservation isn't needed anymore," I challenge them: "Are we really equal now, or are we just pretending because it's more comfortable?"

Here's an interesting point: reservation doesn't just help the direct beneficiaries. It helps *everyone*. Think about it—when marginalized individuals enter the workforce or get an education, they don't just uplift themselves; they enrich society with new perspectives, skills, and experiences. They break cycles of poverty and ignorance, making society more dynamic and forward-thinking.

But the reservation debate doesn't stop there. Some argue for an *economic-based* reservation instead of caste-based ones, and while that idea sounds appealing, it oversimplifies the issue. Caste and class are often intertwined in India. The most disadvantaged communities are usually the ones who also face caste-based discrimination. So, while an economic-based system sounds fair, we must acknowledge that simply focusing on income won't address the root causes of inequality.

Now, let's address the often-heard fear: *Does reservation undermine merit?* Is someone from a reserved category really qualified? Here's the thing—merit doesn't exist in a vacuum. It's shaped by your circumstances. A student from an elite school isn't on the same level as a student from a government school with limited resources. Does that mean the latter is unworthy? Absolutely not. It means they've had to work *much harder* to achieve the same thing, and that's precisely why they deserve a chance too.

So, let's ask ourselves—are we truly starting on equal ground? Or are some people sprinting ahead while others are stuck in the back, fighting uphill against all odds? Reservation isn't about creating unfair advantages—it's about creating an opportunity for everyone to *start* on more equal terms.

Yes, we've discussed a little about this before, but it's important to recognize that reservation is a step toward justice, not a shortcut. It's a tool to correct an *imbalance*, not a permanent crutch. We are demanding fairness, not charity. We're saying that those who have been pushed to the margins of society for generations need a boost—so they can finally be seen as equals in the race for success.

If you still believe reservation is flawed, I want to hear about the society where this has been solved without it. Where is this utopia where everyone, regardless of their background, has had the same chance to succeed? Until we get there, let's not pretend that equality is just a matter of individual effort. It's about addressing the systemic inequalities that persist.

Reservation is not about *privilege*. It's about *correcting an imbalance* that has been in place for centuries. It's about providing everyone with a *real shot* at success. And until we build a society where every single person has the same opportunity, it remains the necessary step forward.

So, let's stop pretending that reservation is unfair. It's not. It's the equalizer we need until we reach a world where no one has to fight for a fair chance at success.

As we dive into the constitutional amendments that address caste-based issues, it's important to recognize that each change is more than just a legal shift—it's a response to the deeper, often painful inequalities that have defined India's social landscape for centuries. These amendments were crafted with the intent to right historical wrongs, but as we'll see, they also spark important conversations about merit, equality, and the complexities of social justice.

Constitutional Amendments and Their Impact

As we dive into the constitutional amendments that address caste-based issues, it's important to recognize that each change is more than just a legal shift—it's a response to the deeper, often painful inequalities that have defined India's social landscape for centuries. These amendments were crafted with the intent to right historical wrongs, but as we'll see, they also spark important conversations about merit, equality, and the complexities of social justice

Take, for example, the **93rd Constitutional Amendment (2005)**. This amendment extended reservations to private educational institutions, marking a critical step in ensuring that access to quality education is not determined by caste or economic status. Under **Article 15(5)**, the amendment allowed for reservations in private unaided institutions, which were previously excluded from affirmative action policies. At first glance, this seems like an undeniable victory. After all, private institutions often offer superior infrastructure, teaching standards, and opportunities. But, real life has shown that even this measure isn't without its complications.

A case that comes to mind is **T.M.A. Pai Foundation v. State of Karnataka (2002)**, a landmark decision by the Supreme Court, which questioned the validity of extending reservations to private educational institutions. The court ruled that while the state could provide reservations, it could not infringe on the autonomy of private institutions. This ruling created a grey area, leaving private educational institutions with the power to either comply or defy the spirit of affirmative action. The 93rd Amendment sought to resolve this ambiguity, but in practice, it has been met with resistance from elite institutions, which argue that reservations compromise academic standards. Yet, we cannot ignore the real-world implications—students from marginalized communities often struggle to gain admission to these institutions due to systemic disadvantages, even though they may have the aptitude and drive to succeed.

This brings us to the **104th Constitutional Amendment (2019)**, which extended reservations for SCs and STs in the Lok Sabha and State Legislative Assemblies. This extension was meant to ensure that marginalized communities continue to have a voice in India's political discourse. But does it go far enough? Take the case of **Mandal Commission Recommendations (1990)**, which had initially recommended reservations in legislatures, and how it sparked widespread protests and debates about the "meritocracy" of our political system. The 104th Amendment's extension might be seen as an attempt to uphold what the Mandal Commission laid out, but the question remains: Is this enough to truly empower marginalized groups politically?

In real life, the impact of these amendments can be observed in both political and social spheres. For instance, political representation for marginalized communities remains a pressing concern. Does the system inadvertently rely too much on caste to define political power?

Moreover, let's consider the **77th Amendment (1995)** and the **81st Amendment (2000)**, which allowed for reservations in promotions for SCs, STs, and OBCs in government jobs. These amendments were necessary to ensure that backward communities were not left behind in career advancements. However, the implementation has often been met with resistance, especially from those in higher government positions who argue that promotions should be based solely on merit. A real-life example is the case of **V. P. Nanjundan v. Union of India (2001)**, in which the Supreme Court upheld the policy of reserving promotions for SCs and STs but also stated that it should be done within a "reasonable" framework to ensure that it doesn't violate the principle of merit.

In practice, though, the policy's application has often led to tensions between those who benefit from it and those who feel excluded. The **anti-reservation protests of 2006**, which erupted in response to the extension of reservations to OBCs in higher education, were a striking example of this tension. Students from the general category saw it as a threat to their opportunities, leading to violent protests across the country. The 93rd Amendment, by providing reservations in private institutions, was an effort to bridge that divide, but it also highlighted the deep societal divides that reservations can inadvertently amplify.

Another relevant amendment, the **92nd Amendment (2003)**, expanded the **Eighth Schedule** to include more languages, further recognizing the diverse cultural identity of India's people. This was an important step in empowering marginalized linguistic communities. But, even here, the question arises: How much does this truly impact caste-based inequalities? Language and culture are deeply intertwined with caste, and often, those from lower castes are subjected to cultural erasure and discrimination. Recognizing linguistic diversity is necessary, but it's not enough to address the root causes of caste discrimination.

Finally, let's step back and look at the larger picture. These amendments have undoubtedly opened doors for marginalized communities—whether through increased representation in education, politics, or employment. Yet, they haven't eliminated caste-based discrimination. The fact that we are still debating the merit of these policies tells us that caste continues to shape access to power and opportunities in India. Take **Bhagwan Das v. Union of India (1995)**, where the court upheld the policy of reservations but also acknowledged the need for change in the way caste was perceived. These cases demonstrate that while affirmative action policies are necessary, they are also a reflection of the deeper challenges we face as a society.

In the end, these constitutional amendments reflect India's commitment to ensuring that the marginalized are not left behind. But as we continue to grapple with issues of caste, merit, and equality, one thing is clear: Legal provisions alone will not undo centuries of inequality. True progress requires a shift in societal attitudes and a rethinking of how we define success and merit. So, as we examine these amendments, let's not just look at them as isolated legal victories. Let's see them for what they are—one part of a much larger, ongoing struggle for a just and equitable society. And the question remains: Are we doing enough, or are we merely scratching the surface? The conversation, I believe, is far from over.

The Living Promise of Equality

The Indian Constitution, in all its brilliance and foresight, laid down the foundation for a nation that could rise above the shackles of caste. It gave us laws, rights, and protections—more than that, it gave us a promise. A promise that no individual would be treated as lesser simply because of the circumstances of their birth. A promise that caste, which once dictated every aspect of a person's existence, would no longer determine their dignity, opportunities, or fate. But let's pause for a moment—has that promise truly been fulfilled?

Laws can be written. Policies can be framed. Courtrooms can deliver judgments. But what happens when society itself resists change? What happens when caste finds new ways to survive—through institutions, through privilege, through silent exclusions that no law can fully capture? What happens when discrimination isn't always explicit but lurks in the shadows of hiring practices, social circles, matrimonial ads, and everyday interactions? The Constitution may have provided the weapons to dismantle caste-based discrimination, but it is up to us to wield them. And if we hesitate, if we choose complacency over confrontation, then we become complicit in the very system we claim to oppose.

The real test of constitutional ideals is not in their existence but in their execution. Policies of reservation and affirmative action were never meant to be mere political tools or temporary concessions—they were meant to correct historical wrongs, to serve as stepping stones toward true equality. But how often do we hear arguments that dismiss them as "unfair advantages" rather than acknowledging them as necessary reparations for centuries of injustice? How often do we see people conveniently declare that "caste no longer matters" while the reality speaks otherwise?

Let's be clear: caste is not just a relic of the past; it is a living, breathing structure that adapts, that persists, that fights to stay relevant even when the law says it shouldn't. If it were truly gone, why do Dalit students still drop out of schools at higher rates due to discrimination? Why do manual scavengers—those forced into inhumane labor for centuries—still exist despite legal bans? Why do we still hear of caste-based violence, honor killings, and social boycotts? If the Constitution was enough on its own, then why do these injustices remain a daily reality for so many?

The truth is, no Constitution, however powerful, can single-handedly erase centuries of conditioning. The law can dictate rights, but it cannot dictate mindsets. That is a battle that must be fought within every home, every school, every workplace, and every conversation. It is a battle that demands uncomfortable discussions, challenges to privilege, and a willingness to see beyond our own lived experiences.

So, where does that leave us? Are we merely spectators, nodding in agreement as we read about constitutional guarantees, or are we willing to be participants in the fight to uphold them? Because caste-based discrimination will not disappear simply because we wish it away. It will end only when society refuses to accept it in any form—when silence is no longer an option, when apathy is no longer excusable, and when justice is no longer conditional on social hierarchy.

The Indian Constitution gave us the map, but the journey is ours to complete. The question is—will we walk the path, or will we abandon it halfway? Because in the end, a nation is not just defined by its laws but by the conviction of its people to uphold them. And until caste is truly dismantled, our work remains unfinished.

Bridging Law and Life

The Indian Constitution has made undeniable strides in confronting caste-based discrimination through well-meaning amendments and judicial interventions. Yet, as we've seen, the letter of the law often falls short of changing the spirit of society. Amendments like the 93rd, 104th, 77th, and others represent powerful commitments to equality, but their implementation has been riddled with tension—between institutional autonomy and social justice, between merit and historical reparation, between legal intention and lived reality.

What these legislative efforts reveal is a deep and ongoing struggle: while the Constitution may light the path, the journey toward equality requires collective societal will. Caste is not merely a legal problem to be solved in courtrooms; it is a social reality entrenched in mindsets, habits, and hierarchies. That is where the true test lies—not in whether laws exist, but in whether they are allowed to work, and whether we, as a people, are ready to confront what still holds us back.

As we move forward, we must ask: Are we willing to live the promise our Constitution makes, not just in statute books but in schools, offices, streets, and homes? Until the idea of equality is felt as much as it is legislated, our constitutional vision remains incomplete. The challenge is not only to preserve the rights enshrined in the Constitution but to bring them fully alive in the everyday lives of all Indians—regardless of caste.

THE IDEALS OF EQUALITY: LESSONS FROM THIRUVALLUVAR

> *"True equality is not in treating all the same, but in recognizing and nurturing the inherent worth in every individual."*

While I may not have the age or experience to fully do justice to Thiruvalluvar, one thing is certain: Thiruvalluvar and his *Thirukural* are inseparable from Tamil culture. Yet, the wisdom embedded in *Thirukural* transcends linguistic and cultural boundaries—its timeless teachings serve as a guiding philosophy for all of humanity, offering valuable principles for living a meaningful life.

Thiruvalluvar and his *Thirukural* aren't just celebrated here in Tamil Nadu—they've been embraced all around the world. You'll find his teachings discussed in universities and cultural events across places like London, New York, Singapore, Malaysia, and Sri Lanka. Even in some parts of Africa, people reflect on the wisdom of *Thirukural.* It's amazing how his words, which have guided Tamil culture for centuries, have found their place in global conversations. Whether it's through academic lectures, cultural festivals, or even philosophy forums, Thiruvalluvar's ideals are being celebrated far and wide. It's proof that his wisdom isn't just for us—it's for everyone, everywhere.

Thiruvalluvar's work, especially the *Thirukural*, is not an exception when it comes to addressing equality. What's truly remarkable is that he wrote these teachings centuries ago, yet they remain incredibly relevant today. His words challenge us to look beyond differences, emphasizing justice, fairness, and respect for all—regardless of caste, creed, or status. In a world still grappling with inequality, *Thirukural* offers timeless wisdom on how to build a more just and equal society, proving that true equality was on his mind long before it became a global conversation.

Equality Beyond Birth and Status

When we talk about equality, especially in the context of birth and status, Thiruvalluvar's voice stands out like a beacon of clarity and wisdom. One of his most revolutionary ideas was the complete rejection of birth-based discrimination. In a time when lineage and caste determined one's place in society, Thiruvalluvar came forward with a thought that was radical, yet profoundly simple. He declared that nobility and virtue are not decided by who your ancestors were, but by who you are as an individual, by the choices you make, and the actions you take in life.

In *Kural 972*, he states:

"Pirapokkum ella uyirkkum"
(All are equal by birth.)

Now, think about this for a moment. This statement, though just a few words, challenges an entire structure that has shaped Indian society for centuries. He's not just saying that all lives are equal, but that equality starts at birth. It's as if Thiruvalluvar is saying, "Regardless of who you're born to, your worth is your own to define." This goes beyond just theory—it speaks to the core of who we are as human beings and how we should treat one another. Thiruvalluvar's call to emphasize individual character over inherited status is a timeless appeal for justice and fairness.

And here's the thing: *Pirapokkum ella uyirkkum* isn't just a philosophical statement; it's a guiding principle for how we should treat each other. It's the blueprint for a society that values each person for who they are, not where they come from. Every action, every interaction, every decision we make—this principle should guide us. Thiruvalluvar's wisdom teaches us that to truly honor the equality of all people, we must treat one another with respect and dignity, regardless of caste, status, or any form of societal division.

In a society where your birth could either open doors or shut them forever, where your identity could be shaped by something beyond your control, Thiruvalluvar's wisdom feels like a breath of fresh air. His words remind us that true nobility lies in how we live our lives, not the family we're born into. And this isn't just some abstract philosophical idea. This principle is the bedrock of fairness, democracy, and social justice.

Let's reflect on how radical this idea was—particularly in the context of India's caste-based system, which for centuries has imposed rigid boundaries, confining people to roles and stations simply because of their birth. Thiruvalluvar spoke against that very notion, urging us to focus on merit—on the actions and qualities that define us as individuals, rather than the circumstances of our birth.

His message wasn't just ahead of its time; it laid the groundwork for countless social reform movements that would follow. Think about the work of Periyar, B.R. Ambedkar, and Mahatma Gandhi. All of these leaders were inspired by the same call for equality that Thiruvalluvar set forth. When we look at these figures, we can see that Thiruvalluvar's ideas weren't just philosophical—they were the foundation of a movement toward social justice, a movement that strives for a society where everyone is recognized for their individual worth, not their ancestry or status.

It's incredible, isn't it? Thiruvalluvar said these things centuries ago, but they speak to us so clearly today. And it's a reminder that true equality is not just a lofty goal—it's something we can achieve, if only we start to look at each other with the same respect and regard that he envisioned.

Justice and Righteous Leadership

When we think about leadership, it's easy to get caught up in images of power and authority. But Thiruvalluvar's definition of leadership is something entirely different. For him, the core of leadership isn't about dominance or personal ambition. It's about *justice*. A leader's true strength is measured by their commitment to fairness, to making sure that every individual—no matter their status, wealth, or birth—receives the respect and equity they deserve.

Thiruvalluvar saw justice as the very foundation of a successful, harmonious society. He didn't see it as a mere abstract concept, but as something that must be actively woven into the fabric of governance. He knew that a ruler who neglects justice, who allows personal biases to cloud their decisions, erodes the trust and stability of the community they serve.

In Kural 541, he states:

"Ezhuvarai thokkadhu neermai yudaiyaan Izhuvarai izhukadhu arasu."
(The just ruler does not abandon the wise and does not oppress the poor.)

Now, let's unpack that. Thiruvalluvar is telling us that true leadership doesn't just respect the wise—it also doesn't exploit the vulnerable. The leader who upholds justice doesn't turn their back on those who offer wisdom, and they don't trample over the poor or powerless. It's about finding that balance—making sure that no one gets left behind, no one gets forgotten, and no one gets unjustly treated.

Think about the world around us today. We hear a lot about justice—equality, fairness, and the rights of the oppressed. But how often do we see that in action? How often do we see leaders prioritizing the welfare of everyone, especially the vulnerable? Thiruvalluvar's call for righteous leadership is a challenge to all of us. It's not just about the big promises politicians make—it's about ensuring that their actions match those promises. It's about making justice the heartbeat of governance, and leadership not as a means to gain power but as a responsibility to uplift others.

When Thiruvalluvar speaks of a just ruler, he's also speaking to each one of us in positions of influence—whether in our communities, our workplaces, or our own families. It's easy to think that leadership is about *doing*—about making decisions and enacting laws. But Thiruvalluvar flips that idea around. Leadership, to him, is about *being*—about embodying justice in every thought, action, and interaction. It's about being the kind of person who treats others with fairness and respect, no matter their background.

And it doesn't stop at the ruler. It's about all of us. Because justice is not just something that we *expect* from our leaders—it's something that we *demand* from ourselves, too. If we truly want to live in a world that mirrors Thiruvalluvar's vision, we need to embody justice in our day-to-day lives. We need to look at the people around us—not as their titles or wealth, but as human beings deserving of the same fairness and dignity we wish for ourselves.

When we look at the world today, his words ring even truer. Leaders in all corners of the world are often judged not by their titles but by their actions. And just as Thiruvalluvar taught us, the essence of leadership lies in the ability to balance wisdom with empathy and justice with compassion. True leadership isn't about how many followers you have—it's about how many lives you touch, how many injustices you correct, and how many people you uplift.

This is where Thiruvalluvar's teachings hold so much weight. His ideas have laid the foundation for modern democratic principles, where equality before the law and the protection of the underprivileged are essential. This is not just something we talk about in theory; it's something that impacts how we engage with the world, how we hold those in power accountable, and how we make sure that everyone—regardless of their station—has a voice.

So, I want you to reflect on this, as I reflect on it too. What does it mean to be a just leader, in your own life? It doesn't matter if you're a student, a parent, a friend, or a boss—each of us has a role in making justice a part of who we are. And in this world, that's what will shape the future. Not the people who sit in power, but the people who lead with their hearts and guide with their actions.

The Dignity of Labor

You know, when we talk about labor—what people do to earn their living or to contribute to society—there's often this invisible hierarchy, isn't there? A quiet system where some jobs are seen as more prestigious than others. And, if we're being honest, this happens all over the world. There's this underlying assumption that certain professions, based on how much money they make or how 'important' they seem, should be valued more than others. But here's the thing—Thiruvalluvar, centuries ago, already understood the value of every single job in society.

He recognized that labor, in all its forms, is an act of dignity. He didn't look at someone sweeping the floor or working in the fields as any less than a ruler or a scholar. Instead, he revered them. He understood that the core of any civilization is built by those who work—whether it's with their hands, their hearts, or their minds.

In Kural 1041, Thiruvalluvar writes:

"Uzhavinar kaithozhil ondru ilan aatrinan Vazhvathul vaazhvadhu ill." (Those who do not engage in any labor contribute nothing to society.)

Let that sink in. No matter how grand your dreams are or how far you go in life, if you don't contribute in some way, if you don't roll up your sleeves and get your hands dirty (literally or figuratively), you're not really making an impact. You're not building anything meaningful. Thiruvalluvar doesn't talk down on those who perform manual labor—he elevates them. He says their contribution is just as vital as anyone else's, and in fact, without their hard work, the entire structure of society would crumble.

I want to tell you a story that really got me thinking about this. It's about a man I met when I was younger. I was visiting my grandfather's village, and there was this elderly man who worked as a gardener. He wasn't rich—didn't own any land or have any fancy titles. But every morning, I would watch him wake up at dawn and go about his work with such care, planting flowers and tending to the trees. One day, I asked him why he was so dedicated to his work, even though nobody really noticed him.

He looked at me and said, "What good is a garden if it's not cared for? If no one takes the time to water the plants or trim the bushes, it dies. So, I do it every day. Not for praise, but because I believe in what I'm doing."

That hit me hard. Here was a man who wasn't doing his job for anyone's approval. He wasn't chasing wealth or fame—he was simply fulfilling his role in the world with the kind of integrity that was rare to see. And his work was beautiful. It added value to the community, even though it was simple and, to some, maybe even menial.

Thiruvalluvar would have celebrated this man. Because for him, *every* form of labor was worthy of respect. The gardener, the teacher, the driver, the farmer—all these people make society tick. They are the unsung heroes. In his time, and in ours, there are countless invisible workers who give their best without recognition. And that's why Thiruvalluvar's words are so timely and timeless. They remind us to recognize the dignity in every task. Not just the tasks that seem grand but the quiet, often overlooked work that holds everything together.

Take a moment and think about it. How often do we overlook the workers who clean our streets, serve our food, or fix our cars? The truth is, we've all had moments where we've taken these tasks for granted. But imagine if all the workers in society stopped doing their jobs—imagine if the farmers stopped growing food, the janitors stopped cleaning, the electricians stopped fixing wires. Society would come to a standstill. Yet, these are the very people who rarely get the recognition they deserve.

Thiruvalluvar would never let us forget that. He would ask us to take a step back and honor the labor of all. He'd remind us that *true* dignity lies in the integrity with which we perform our tasks. It's not about the status attached to the job; it's about the heart with which you approach it.

I also think of the great social reformers like B.R. Ambedkar and Mahatma Gandhi. Ambedkar fought against caste-based discrimination, where certain jobs were considered inferior because of the caste into which someone was born. Gandhi, too, championed manual labor through his concept of Sarvodaya, which held that manual work was sacred and should be revered, not devalued. Both of them fought for the dignity of all workers and fought to erase the caste-based division of labor.

Thiruvalluvar's message goes hand-in-hand with these ideas. He was telling us that no matter who you are or what job you do, you have intrinsic worth. Your work contributes to the whole of society, and that is something to be proud of.

So, how do we take this message into our lives today? It's about looking at the world around us with new eyes—seeing every worker, every profession, with respect. Whether someone is working in a hospital, in a factory, or on the streets, they're all playing an essential part in the functioning of society. Next time you see someone doing their job, remember Thiruvalluvar's wisdom. Don't look at them as 'less than,' but as someone who, in their own unique way, is contributing to the greater good.

If we all start viewing labor through this lens of respect and dignity, maybe we can build a society that not only values work but values the people who perform it. And just maybe, we can all look at the world with a little more gratitude for those unsung heroes who quietly make everything possible.

Compassion and Brotherhood

Let's take a moment and think about the world we live in today—how often do we find ourselves in situations where compassion feels like a rare commodity? Life's pace, the rush, and sometimes our own egos make us forget the very essence of what connects us all—love and respect. Thiruvalluvar, though, he got it right—centuries ago.

He didn't just talk about legal and social equality—he understood that true harmony goes beyond laws. It's about how we *treat* each other on a daily basis, in our interactions and in our communities. He believed that at the heart of any great society is compassion and that the way we approach others shapes the world we live in.

In Kural 25, Thiruvalluvar says:

"Anbu udaimai arane naadi Thinbum thakarkkum perum."
(Possession of love is the greatest virtue, as it eradicates suffering.)

This simple yet profound verse brings us back to the core of humanity—love, empathy, and kindness. It's as if he's telling us, "If you want to end suffering, if you want peace, then lead with love. Show compassion."

What strikes me about Thiruvalluvar's message is how it transcends time. Think about the world we live in today—despite all the advancements, technology, and progress, there's a lack of true compassion in many aspects of life. People are caught up in their own lives, competing with each other, often forgetting the importance of brotherhood, of looking out for one another.

But Thiruvalluvar, he tells us that compassion is the greatest virtue. It's bigger than wealth, bigger than status, bigger than any title. It's the foundation of a society that works in harmony. He advocates for a world where we treat one another with kindness, where we don't let arrogance, pride, or prejudice blind us from seeing the humanity in others.

Think about how different the world could be if we truly embraced this idea. Can you imagine a society where everyone, regardless of their background, was treated with respect, where people cared about each other's well-being? A society where the strong lifted the weak, and no one was left behind. That's the kind of world Thiruvalluvar envisioned—a world where compassion and brotherhood are the guiding principles.

This teaching is so relevant today, don't you think? Look around, and you'll see that we still struggle with issues like inequality, prejudice, and discrimination. Whether it's based on caste, gender, race, or any other divide, we still see these cracks in society. But imagine, just for a moment, if we took Thiruvalluvar's words to heart—if we made compassion a daily practice, something that guides us in every interaction, no matter how small.

There's a story I want to share that really made me think of Thiruvalluvar's teachings on compassion. It's about a time when I was volunteering for a social initiative, helping to distribute food and supplies to those in need. We were at a busy market, and while everyone else was rushing around, there was an elderly woman sitting by herself. She looked lost, and no one seemed to notice her. I walked over to her, and as I sat beside her and spoke to her, she shared how lonely she felt. She had no family around and felt invisible in the crowd.

That moment hit me. The world had moved on without even pausing to notice this woman, yet all she needed was a little compassion. Just someone to see her, to acknowledge her pain. I realized that, in that brief interaction, I had the power to make a difference—not by giving her money or gifts, but by showing her that she mattered.

This is exactly what Thiruvalluvar means when he talks about the power of love. It doesn't always have to be grand gestures. Sometimes, it's the small acts of kindness that can have the most profound impact on someone's life.

Thiruvalluvar's focus on compassion goes hand-in-hand with his idea of fraternity. Brotherhood is not about belonging to a specific group or community. It's about seeing every human being as part of the larger whole. When we practice compassion, we acknowledge that the struggles of others are our struggles, their joys are our joys, and that we are all connected by this thread of humanity.

In a way, compassion is the glue that holds us together. It's easy to get caught up in our own little worlds, especially in times of stress or when we're focused on our goals. But if we can take a step back and remember that the people around us are also navigating their own challenges, it shifts our perspective. Compassion doesn't just enrich the lives of others—it enriches our own.

If you think about the teachings of great leaders like Martin Luther King Jr., Mahatma Gandhi, or even modern advocates for human rights, they all echo the same sentiment. They fought for justice, for equality, but they also fought for love, for compassion, for the dignity of every individual. And this is exactly what Thiruvalluvar was teaching us centuries ago.

So, let's carry this lesson forward. Let's remind ourselves, every day, that love and compassion should be at the heart of our actions. That brotherhood isn't just about standing together when it's easy, but supporting one another through the tough times. Imagine the change we could create in our world, simply by choosing to be a little kinder, a little more understanding.

That's the power of Thiruvalluvar's wisdom. His vision of a compassionate, harmonious world is something we can still strive toward today.

Relevance in Contemporary Society

You know, it's fascinating how the teachings of Thiruvalluvar have managed to stand the test of time. We're talking about centuries of history, yet the core values he laid out for us continue to resonate. In a world where social inequalities are still so prevalent—be it caste, race, gender, or economic status—his teachings are not just relevant, but essential. They serve as a reminder of the values we should be living by, values that often seem to get lost in the hustle of modern life.

I want you to think for a second: Why, in a time where we are more connected than ever, do we still see these divides? Why do caste-based biases continue to harm millions, why do racial prejudices still haunt societies, and why do economic disparities keep people in chains? The question seems simple, yet the answer is complex. Thiruvalluvar, however, gives us a roadmap.

His emphasis on justice, merit, and human dignity provides a much-needed anchor in today's sea of confusion. His philosophy doesn't just sound good—it challenges us to reflect, to change the way we interact with others, and to reform systems that perpetuate inequality. The kind of society Thiruvalluvar envisioned, one where everyone is treated with fairness, dignity, and respect, is not a pipe dream—it's one that we're still striving for, and his teachings can guide us through that journey.

I often think about how closely Thiruvalluvar's teachings align with the fundamental principles of equality that we find in modern constitutions—principles that state that every individual should have the same rights, should be treated equally before the law, and should not be discriminated against based on arbitrary factors like birth or background. It's almost as if Thiruvalluvar was laying down the moral foundation for those very ideals centuries ago. And it's not just about laws—it's about us, the individuals, living those principles every day.

And then, if we look at the global struggles for justice today, we can see the direct impact of his message. Take the anti-apartheid movement in South Africa, led by Nelson Mandela. The fight against racial injustice was rooted in the very principles Thiruvalluvar advocated—equality, respect, and dignity for all people, regardless of their race or background. It wasn't just about fighting laws—it was about fighting a mindset that sought to undermine the worth of human beings based on the color of their skin. And it wasn't just a political struggle—it was a battle for humanity.

Similarly, think of the Dalit rights movement in India, led by leaders like Dr. B.R. Ambedkar. Thiruvalluvar's words would have resonated deeply with Ambedkar, as he sought to challenge the social structures that oppressed millions based on their caste. Ambedkar, too, believed in the idea of social justice, where no individual's worth is determined by their caste or birth but by their actions and merit. Thiruvalluvar's philosophy is still alive in these movements—his wisdom continues to inspire those who fight for equality.

But here's the thing: These struggles aren't just happening in history books—they're still unfolding. We see it in the movements today. In fact, we see it every time someone stands up for the rights of the marginalized, every time someone speaks out against injustice, and every time someone questions the systems that hold us back. The beauty of Thiruvalluvar's teachings is that they empower us to be a part of that change. They don't just ask us to hope for a better world—they ask us to build one ourselves.

I remember a conversation I had with a friend about the caste-based discrimination that still exists today. We were discussing how it manifests in subtle ways in modern-day India—how the system of privilege continues to perpetuate itself, despite legal progress. My friend, who had recently visited South Africa, shared a story about how people there still talk about the impact of apartheid in their communities. It wasn't just a legal system that was defeated—it was a mindset, a deeply ingrained belief that some lives were less valuable than others. And even today, generations later, those scars remain. But they also continue to fuel movements for change. The struggles of the past are not forgotten—they become the driving force for a future where dignity and justice are accessible to all.

So, how do we carry Thiruvalluvar's message forward? We take it into our daily lives. We reject the prejudices that have been handed down to us. We question the systems that perpetuate inequality. We strive to treat every single person with the respect and dignity they deserve. It's not about being a passive spectator in the face of injustice—it's about actively participating in the creation of a more just world. And that's exactly what Thiruvalluvar was calling us to do.

We are the generation that must take his ideals and live them out. The struggles of the past should inspire us, but they should also challenge us to do better, to be better. Thiruvalluvar's vision of a just and compassionate society can still be realized, if we choose to make it happen. It's not about waiting for someone else to lead the way—it's about each of us taking responsibility for creating a world that reflects the values of equality, justice, and compassion that Thiruvalluvar taught us.

Legal and Constitutional Alignment

When I reflect on the deep wisdom of **Thiruvalluvar**, I'm always struck by how timeless and far-reaching his ideas are. It's almost as if his words were not just a product of their time but were meant to guide us into the future. The more I learn about the **Indian Constitution**, the more I see the profound connection between the ideals of **Thiruvalluvar** and the legal foundation of our country.

Take a moment to consider the **Indian Constitution**. You'll see that it is built on the very principles that Thiruvalluvar laid down centuries ago. **Articles 14-17**, which ensure equality before the law and prohibit discrimination on the grounds of caste, race, religion, or sex, align seamlessly with what Thiruvalluvar advocated. His message that all individuals should be judged by their actions and not by their birth resonates strongly in the very DNA of the Indian Constitution.

I want you to picture this: a nation coming together, after the turmoil of colonial rule, to write a document that promises equality and justice for all its citizens. In **Kural 972**, Thiruvalluvar says, *"Pirapokkum ella uyirkkum"* (All are equal by birth). Now, let's bring this into the context of the Constitution. The very fact that every citizen of India, regardless of their background, is guaranteed equality before the law is a direct reflection of Thiruvalluvar's ideology. Just like Thiruvalluvar imagined a society based on merit, the Constitution promises a society where each individual's worth is measured by their actions, not by their caste or class.

It's fascinating when you think about how **Thiruvalluvar's** verses from centuries ago seem to echo in modern-day India. In **Article 15** of the Constitution, it states that the state shall not discriminate against any citizen on the grounds of religion, race, caste, sex, or place of birth. Isn't that an embodiment of Thiruvalluvar's call for equality and fairness? His verses acted as a moral compass that laid the foundation for the very rights we hold dear today.

Now, let's take a step further and think about **social justice**. The **Directive Principles of State Policy** enshrined in the Indian Constitution also reflect Thiruvalluvar's call for a just society. These principles guide the state towards securing a fair and just society for all, with a focus on improving the welfare of its people. Thiruvalluvar's teachings, with their emphasis on fairness, go hand-in-hand with these constitutional principles.

I want to share an interesting story here. Have you ever heard of the way **B.R. Ambedkar**, the principal architect of the Indian Constitution, was inspired by the teachings of various reformers who fought against caste-based oppression? Thiruvalluvar was one of those reformers. Ambedkar, who dedicated his life to breaking caste barriers and ensuring equality for Dalits and other marginalized communities, was deeply moved by thinkers like Thiruvalluvar, who envisioned a society where birth had no bearing on one's worth.

Ambedkar's philosophy of **annihilation of caste** was a direct challenge to the deep-seated caste system in India, just as Thiruvalluvar's verses had been centuries before. Ambedkar believed that caste-based discrimination was the root cause of social injustice, and Thiruvalluvar's teachings of equality provided him with a moral framework to support his fight for a just society.

There's a remarkable moment I want to highlight. Ambedkar, after drafting the Constitution, went on record saying that **equality** is the "first and the most important" principle for any nation. This idea, he emphasized, could not be achieved without breaking down caste barriers and ensuring that no one is judged by their birth. It's almost as if Ambedkar was continuing the work that Thiruvalluvar had started. When Ambedkar drafted the Constitution, he ensured that the ideals of equality, justice, and merit were embedded within it, making it a living document that reflects the vision of thinkers like Thiruvalluvar.

As I think about the **Constitution's vision of equality**, I can't help but feel the resonance with Thiruvalluvar's profound words. In many ways, his teachings were a roadmap, guiding the leaders of modern India in their struggle to create a just and fair society. And today, as we continue to grapple with issues of caste, race, and discrimination, we can turn to both the **Constitution** and **Thiruvalluvar** as guiding lights, reminding us that true equality is not just a legal principle, but a moral imperative.

You know, it's fascinating to see how **Thiruvalluvar's** teachings weren't just ahead of their time—they were far-reaching in their scope. His advocacy for a society where all individuals are treated equally is not just a principle; it's a vision. And as we continue to face challenges in the fight for social justice, his words remain just as relevant now as they were thousands of years ago.

Let's ask ourselves: **How far have we come?** We have the Constitution, we have Ambedkar's framework, but are we living up to the ideals that Thiruvalluvar and Ambedkar envisioned? The fight for equality, justice, and meritocracy continues, and it's up to each of us to ensure that these principles aren't just written in law but are lived and breathed in our everyday lives.

Thiruvalluvar and Global Social Justice

When we delve into the world of **Thiruvalluvar**, it's easy to assume that his teachings are limited to **Tamil culture** or even **Indian society**. But what if I told you that the essence of his philosophy is far more **universal**, transcending **time** and **geography**? Let's take a step back and explore how his profound wisdom extends beyond our borders, echoing the values that have shaped some of the most important social justice movements around the globe.

Now, think for a moment about **Confucius**—one of the most influential philosophers in Chinese history. What do we know about him? **Confucius** was firm in his belief that **birthright** should never define a person's worth. Instead, he argued that it is **virtue**—one's actions and morality—that shapes a person's value. This resonates deeply with **Thiruvalluvar's vision**, especially when we reflect on his famous Kural 972: *"Pirapokkum ella uyirkkum"* (All are equal by birth). Isn't it striking how both thinkers, from entirely different parts of the world, emphasize the same truth: **nobility comes from virtue, not lineage**?

This isn't just ancient wisdom, by the way. It's **timeless**, as relevant today as it was thousands of years ago. Think of it like this: We live in a world where **social mobility** is still a struggle for so many. Where **wealth** and **status** sometimes determine the opportunities available to us. And yet, in the very bones of humanity, there's this incredible truth: your worth isn't defined by where you come from, but by **who you choose to be**. It's like **Confucius** and **Thiruvalluvar** were both whispering the same message, across centuries and continents, urging us to rise above birth, status, and circumstance.

Now let's turn our gaze to **John Locke**, the **English philosopher** who helped lay the groundwork for modern **democracy**. Locke argued that every person is born with certain **inalienable rights**—the right to **life**,

liberty, and **property**. And if we look at **Thiruvalluvar's** ideas on **equality**, **justice**, and **merit**, we can see an immediate parallel. Both thinkers are advocating for a society where **individuals** are seen as **equal**, where **justice** is blind to birth or caste, and where everyone has an equal shot at life, based on their **merit**.

Here's the thing—when I think about **Locke** and **Thiruvalluvar**, I can't help but marvel at how their visions are strikingly similar. Both talked about **natural rights**, the idea that **every individual** deserves **dignity** and **respect**, no matter their background. It's a **common thread** that runs through their works, woven together by the belief in **justice** as the cornerstone of society. It's like the world's **great minds** were all saying, "This is the way to a better world"—and Thiruvalluvar's ideas were ahead of their time, pointing toward a future where **everyone is treated equally**, with **respect** and **fairness**.

And you know what makes all of this even more fascinating? Thiruvalluvar's principles aren't just **theoretical**—they have had **real-world applications** across **social movements** that sought to break down **discrimination** and **oppression**.

Take the **American Civil Rights Movement**, for example. Leaders like **Martin Luther King Jr.** fought against racial inequality, a system that kept millions of people in chains simply because of the color of their skin. His iconic "I Have a Dream" speech wasn't just about **freedom**; it was about **justice** and **equality**—values that Thiruvalluvar championed centuries before. King's dream of a world where people would be **judged by the content of their character** echoes the very heart of **Thiruvalluvar's** teachings.

And it doesn't stop there. The same call for **equality**, **dignity**, and **human rights** has resonated across other social justice struggles, from **India's Dalit rights movement** to the **anti-apartheid movement** in

South Africa. Think of **Nelson Mandela**, who fought for racial equality, or **B.R. Ambedkar**, who stood for the **rights of Dalits** in India. In their struggles, they were echoing **Thiruvalluvar's** fundamental belief that **human dignity** should never be tied to one's **birth**, **caste**, or **race**. **Thiruvalluvar's ideals**, as much as they were rooted in the **Tamil context**, **flourished globally**, fueling **movements for social justice** all over the world.

But here's the thing I want to bring to you today—**Thiruvalluvar's teachings are not just for activists, philosophers, or world leaders**. His philosophy is for **each of us**, for you and me, in our everyday lives. It's in the choices we make, the way we treat each other, and the values we uphold in our communities. In a world where inequality still exists, Thiruvalluvar's message reminds us that **the fight for justice** isn't just something that happened in the past—it's something we need to **keep fighting for**.

So, when you look at your own life, at your family, your friends, and even strangers around you, ask yourself: **How can we embody these values of justice**, **compassion**, and **equality**? How can we break down **social barriers**—whether they're based on **race**, **caste**, or **gender**—and create a society where everyone has a chance to thrive?

I'll tell you this: If we can bring a little more of Thiruvalluvar's wisdom into our hearts and minds, if we can remember that **we are all equal**, no matter where we come from, then perhaps, just perhaps, we might create the kind of world that **Thiruvalluvar** envisioned all those centuries ago—a world where **love**, **respect**, and **justice** rule the day.

Thiruvalluvar's Legacy: A Blueprint for Global Harmony

As we wrap up our journey through the timeless wisdom of Thiruvalluvar, one thing becomes clear: his legacy is not bound by time or geography. His vision for a just, compassionate, and equitable society isn't just a theory—it's a practical framework that can guide our actions, both on a personal level and within the wider scope of society. His teachings stand as a blueprint for global harmony, offering not only moral guidance but also a foundation for transformative change.

Thiruvalluvar believed that true greatness in any society is reflected in the equality of its people, irrespective of their birth, status, or wealth. He understood that when we treat others with fairness and kindness, we foster an environment where every individual has the opportunity to flourish. This idea is as relevant today as it was centuries ago, particularly in a world still grappling with issues of inequality, discrimination, and prejudice.

Consider this: In many ways, Thiruvalluvar was ahead of his time, advocating for principles that align with global movements for social justice. From the civil rights struggles in the United States to the anti-caste movements in India, his teachings have resonated with reformers, activists, and lawmakers alike. His emphasis on **individual merit** over **birthright** has inspired legal systems that prioritize equality under the law, irrespective of one's background. Think of it as the very foundation on which movements like gender equality, racial justice, and economic reform are built.

Take, for instance, the story of **Nelson Mandela**. In his pursuit of a just and equal society in South Africa, Mandela not only fought against apartheid but also advocated for the values of reconciliation, justice, and human dignity—principles that Thiruvalluvar championed. Mandela's vision of a **rainbow nation** echoes Thiruvalluvar's call for unity and respect among all people, showing how deeply Thiruvalluvar's message has shaped leaders worldwide.

In today's context, embracing Thiruvalluvar's principles can guide the **legal and political systems** of every nation toward fairness, equality, and justice. Just like John Locke's ideas helped shape modern democracy, Thiruvalluvar's vision of equality can inform today's **global human rights agenda**. His teachings provide a roadmap for societies striving for **social reform**—reminding us that true progress is only possible when we move beyond divisions and focus on **our shared humanity**.

The global relevance of Thiruvalluvar's wisdom offers a deep reflection on what kind of world we wish to build. **A world where each individual, irrespective of race, gender, caste, or nationality, can live with dignity.** This is not just an ideal; it is a possibility. And as we reflect on his teachings, we should be reminded that the path to this world starts with us—each one of us, upholding his values in our everyday lives, decisions, and interactions.

So, as we conclude, let's ask ourselves: What kind of world are we building for future generations? A world where inequality and discrimination are the norm, or one where compassion, fairness, and equality reign supreme? Thiruvalluvar gave us the **blueprint**, and it's up to us to follow it—now, and forever.

KEY REPRESENTATION OF LEADERS

"At every turn, we choose the paths of leaders who inspire change, embody resilience, and carry the hopes of the unheard."

Leaders without whom none of us would have come all the way, without whom our struggle for equality could not have been won, or at least been made liberal. Especially today, if I am able to write a book on this, it can never be without them—from past leaders to the present.

Leadership in India has been deeply intertwined with the country's historical, social, and political evolution. The leaders who have emerged over time have not only shaped policy and governance but have also played a critical role in addressing caste dynamics, social justice, and economic reforms. This chapter delves into the key figures who have significantly impacted India's caste-based political landscape and how their ideologies continue to shape contemporary politics.

Who should we begin with? Should it be the man himself, Dr. B.R. Ambedkar, the architect of social justice? Or the man who stood with the oppressed, Mahatma Gandhi? Perhaps the pioneers of education and equality, Jyotirao Phule and Savitribai Phule, who laid the foundation for social reform? Or should we start with my hero, Periyar, the key reason many of us today no longer carry our caste names as identities? Maybe the Dravidian and socialist leaders who shaped modern politics deserve the first mention. Or should we turn to the global revolutionaries—Nelson Mandela, Martin Luther King Jr., Che Guevara, and Karl Marx—whose ideas have influenced struggles for equality and justice worldwide?

Dr. B.R. Ambedkar: The Architect of Social Justice

If there is one man without whom many of us wouldn't have the right to dream, let alone fight for it, it is **Dr. B.R. Ambedkar**. He wasn't just a leader. He was a revolution. A storm that refused to be silenced. A man who stood not only for himself but for every soul chained by the shackles of caste. Today, if we walk into institutions, sit in classrooms, and voice our opinions without someone reminding us of our place in an oppressive social order, it is because of him. But do we truly understand what it took for him to get us here?

Imagine this—young Bhimrao, a boy born into the so-called 'untouchable' Mahar caste, sitting in a classroom, thirsty. The well was right there, but he couldn't drink from it. The teachers wouldn't touch his books. He had to sit on a gunny sack, away from his privileged classmates. Even the peon had to pour water into his hands from a distance, as if he was impure, unworthy of even touching the vessel. Now, imagine that boy growing up, leaving behind this country of discrimination, and entering Columbia University and the London School of Economics, where he became one of the greatest minds of his time. He returned—not for revenge, but for justice. For his people. For all of us.

Dr. Ambedkar wasn't just fighting against caste. He was fighting a system that made people believe they were less than human. He saw independence not as the end of the struggle but as the beginning of a bigger war—the fight for **real freedom**. Because what is political freedom if a person still cannot enter a temple? What is democracy if it is built on the suffering of the oppressed?

Ambedkar's Vision: A Radical Change in Society

Dr. Ambedkar's vision was crystal clear: the dismantling of the caste system and the building of a society based on equality, justice, and fraternity. He didn't just want social reforms within the existing system; he wanted a complete overhaul of the foundations of Indian society, which he saw as deeply entrenched in inequality.

Ambedkar understood that real liberation could never come unless the caste system, which had relegated millions to a life of untouchability and oppression, was eradicated. His call wasn't just for social justice; it was for an entirely new framework of social relations. This was a man who not only led the Dalits out of the shadows but also fought for their place in the modern Indian state. His speeches, writings, and legal reforms all pushed for a radical transformation — not just of laws, but of the very structures that had perpetuated social discrimination for centuries.

But here's the thing: Dr. Ambedkar wasn't just a fiery revolutionary. He was also a scholar, an intellectual who understood the complexities of the task ahead. His vision wasn't built on idealism alone. He was practical, and this practicality often placed him in positions of conflict and contradiction.

The Radical vs. The Realist: Ambedkar's Struggle for a New India

Dr. Ambedkar's radical approach to caste abolition often came into tension with the more gradual, reformist strategies of figures like Gandhi. While Gandhi, with his belief in non-violence and gradual change, tried to reform the caste system from within, Ambedkar sought to obliterate it entirely.

Take, for example, the question of separate electorates for Dalits. Gandhi, who believed in unity and non-violence, opposed separate electorates, fearing that it would divide Hindus further. Gandhi's belief in integrating Dalits into mainstream society was driven by his vision of a united India, but he failed to understand the deep pain of the Dalit community, who had been victims of centuries of exclusion. Ambedkar, on the other hand, saw separate electorates as the only way for Dalits to have a political voice in a society that had historically ignored their needs.

Their disagreement over this issue reached its peak during the Poona Pact of 1932, where Gandhi went on a hunger strike in protest of separate electorates for Dalits. The outcome was a compromise that diluted Ambedkar's demands, but Ambedkar's frustration was evident. He believed that Gandhi's paternalism was not a solution; it was merely a temporary measure to placate the caste system rather than dismantling it.

Ambedkar and Hinduism: The Search for a New Identity

One of the most striking contradictions in Ambedkar's life was his relationship with Hinduism. Ambedkar was born a Hindu, but he was a Hindu who was deeply disillusioned with the religion. He had seen the oppressive structures of caste play out in the temples, the streets, and in every corner of society. Ambedkar's critique of Hinduism was both philosophical and personal. He believed that Hinduism, with its deeply ingrained caste hierarchy, was incompatible with his ideals of justice and equality.

So, in 1956, Ambedkar made a radical decision that shook the foundations of Indian society — he embraced Buddhism, taking thousands of Dalits along with him in a mass conversion. This was not just a religious conversion; it was a political statement. Ambedkar wanted to show the world that Dalits didn't need to adhere to a religion that had oppressed them for centuries. He sought refuge in Buddhism, a religion that he saw as offering equality, freedom, and a path to liberation.

Yet, despite his break from Hinduism, Ambedkar's relationship with religion remained complicated. His views on religion were complex — while he rejected the institutionalized structures of Hinduism, he didn't outright dismiss spirituality. Ambedkar believed in the power of reason, but he also understood the role that religion could play in transforming people's hearts and minds. His relationship with religion, like many aspects of his life, was not straightforward. It was a blend of reason, rebellion, and a deep desire for social and political transformation.

Ambedkar's Struggles with His Own People

Another dimension of Ambedkar's life that often goes unexamined is his relationship with the Dalit community itself. While he is seen as the savior of Dalits, his journey wasn't without internal struggles. Ambedkar was often frustrated with the lack of unity among Dalits, who were not always willing to stand up against the oppressive caste system. He saw them as being too absorbed in their day-to-day survival to recognize the broader struggle for liberation.

Ambedkar's frustration with the Dalit community was evident in his speeches and writings. He criticized the Dalit leadership for being timid and for seeking acceptance from the higher castes rather than challenging the very system that had enslaved them. He didn't just want to be a leader of Dalits; he wanted them to recognize their potential and power to create change. Ambedkar's call for Dalit unity was often met with resistance, and this struggle within his own community was a recurring theme in his life.

Ambedkar's Legacy: A Vision Realized, But Not Without Compromise

When we think of Dr. Ambedkar today, we often see him as a figure of towering intellect and moral clarity. His work on the Indian Constitution was groundbreaking, and his advocacy for the marginalized continues to inspire movements for social justice around the world. But Ambedkar was not a man without contradictions. His relationship with religion, his political battles with Gandhi, and his internal struggles with his own community show that his vision for change was not always clear-cut or universally accepted.

And this, I think, is what makes Ambedkar such a compelling figure. Like Gandhi, he was a man driven by ideals — ideals that were sometimes at odds with the realities he faced. He was a radical, yes, but also a pragmatist. He was a revolutionary, but he also understood the delicate art of negotiation. Ambedkar's life, much like the society he sought to change, was filled with complexities.

His legacy is one of uncompromising commitment to justice, but also of deep human vulnerability. Ambedkar was a man who saw the world as it was, and rather than retreating from the darkness, he chose to confront it head-on. His contradictions, far from diminishing his legacy, enrich it — for in those contradictions, we see the true depth of his vision and the profound challenges he faced in his quest for a just society.

He **did not beg for justice; he demanded it**. As the chairman of the Drafting Committee of the Indian Constitution, he ensured that the law would no longer be written by those in power to serve themselves. He gave us the tools to fight back—reservations, anti-discrimination laws, and the fundamental right to equality. But do we even realize how much resistance he faced?

When Ambedkar demanded separate electorates for Dalits, he was met with hostility, even from those who claimed to fight for freedom. The **Poona Pact of 1932** was forced upon him, denying Dalits the right to their own political representation. He accepted it, not because he was weak, but because he knew that a real battle is fought in the long run. And he never stopped fighting.

One of his greatest works, *Annihilation of Caste*, was never even delivered as a speech because the people who invited him couldn't handle the truth he spoke. They wanted reform, but only as long as it didn't shake the very foundations of caste privilege. But Ambedkar didn't need a stage. His words became a movement. His ideals live on.

Today, when we talk about rights, reservations, or even basic dignity, we owe it to him. Yet, how many of us truly understand what he stood for? He once said, *"I measure the progress of a community by the degree of progress which women have achieved."* He didn't just fight for Dalits; he fought for **women, workers, and every oppressed individual**. His idea of justice was not limited—it was universal.

Even towards the end of his life, when he embraced Buddhism in 1956, it was not an escape. It was a rejection of a system that refused to let him, or his people, live with dignity. He **chose** his own path, proving that the greatest revolution is the one where you refuse to accept the chains they give you.

So, let me ask you this—do we still remember him as the man who gave us the Constitution? Or do we remember him as the man who gave us **the courage to fight, the vision to question, and the right to exist with dignity?** Because if we don't, we are failing him.

Mahatma Gandhi: The Reformer with Contradictions

When we think of Mahatma Gandhi, we often think of the man who led a nation towards independence with his philosophy of non-violence and truth. He is revered not only for his fight against British colonialism but also for his bold ideas on social reform, his love for simplicity, and his deep belief in moral discipline. But as we look closer, we see a complex figure, a man who was deeply entrenched in contradictions.

Gandhi was a man of profound vision, yet one whose thoughts and actions were often at odds with the world he sought to shape. His life and philosophy provide us with a deep lesson on the complexities of social and political change, and as we reflect on his legacy, we might find ourselves grappling with some tough questions.

Let's pause for a moment and ask ourselves: **Who was Gandhi, really?** Was he the selfless saint we have been taught about, or was he a reformer with his own set of contradictions that make him more human, and in some ways, more relatable?

The Reformer: Gandhi's Vision for a New India

Let's begin by acknowledging what Gandhi did that continues to inspire millions. His philosophy of non-violence (*ahimsa*) and truth (*satya*) isn't just political rhetoric; it's a lifestyle. Gandhi wasn't merely advocating for independence from British rule; he was pushing for a total transformation of society — a shift in how we, as individuals and communities, interact with each other. His methods — civil disobedience, non-violent protests, and peaceful resistance — were revolutionary in their own right.

Gandhi took the fight to the British Empire in ways that no one had imagined before. One of the most iconic stories is the Salt March — when Gandhi, in 1930, walked 240 miles to the sea to make salt, defying the

British monopoly on it. It wasn't just about salt; it was about reclaiming the power and dignity of a nation. And it wasn't just a political statement; it was a profound act of resistance that involved every ordinary Indian, from peasants to intellectuals.

But Gandhi didn't stop there. He understood that a free India was not just about achieving political independence. It was about freeing the hearts and minds of the people. His work to eradicate untouchability, to uplift women, and to promote rural self-reliance were part of a broader vision of a just and equal society.

The Contradictions: Gandhi's Complex Legacy

And yet, as much as we revere his achievements, we cannot ignore the contradictions within his philosophy and actions.

Take, for instance, Gandhi's stance on modernity and industrialization: On one hand, he advocated for rural development, promoting the spinning of khadi as a symbol of self-reliance and resistance to British goods. He believed in a simple, self-sustained life, detached from the materialism and industrialization that he saw as corrupting society. Gandhi's call to reject Western industrial progress is inspiring in many ways, but it also led to criticisms — some even argue that this rejection stunted India's industrial growth, leaving it struggling in the post-independence era.

But perhaps the most difficult contradictions lie in his views on women and the caste system.

Gandhi's Views on Women: Progressive or Paternalistic?

Gandhi's relationship with the idea of women's emancipation is, in many ways, a testament to how progressive ideas can coexist with deeply traditional beliefs. He advocated for women's involvement in the independence struggle, asking them to take on leadership roles in the national movement. But while he spoke about women's strength and resilience, he simultaneously held onto ideas that were deeply rooted in the past. His views on women's roles — particularly in marriage and family life — were conventional by today's standards. For Gandhi, a woman's primary duty was to maintain purity, chastity, and domesticity, often at the expense of her individual agency.

He also believed that women should embody the values of non-violence and should be the moral conscience of society. While this sounds empowering in theory, it was also incredibly restrictive. Gandhi saw women as the guardians of societal virtue, but in doing so, he confined them to certain roles that left little room for individual freedom.

I can't help but reflect on this contradiction and think: was Gandhi, in his quest for purity and non-violence, placing women on a pedestal — or was he, in fact, diminishing their independence?

The Caste System: A Struggle for Reform or Reform Within Limits?

Gandhi's work against untouchability, his efforts to improve the conditions of the "Harijans," is well-known. He famously called them the "children of God" and dedicated much of his life to fighting their social ostracization. But Gandhi's approach to the caste system was one of reform, not abolition. His idea of removing untouchability within the confines of the caste system itself was progressive, yet it didn't challenge the very foundation of caste. Gandhi was willing to dismantle the most brutal aspects of the caste system but was hesitant to question its hierarchical structure entirely.

It's easy to admire Gandhi's commitment to social justice, but I can't help but wonder — could his message have been more radical? Could he have envisioned a society completely free from caste-based discrimination, rather than trying to "reform" a system that, by its very nature, entrenched inequality?

The Gandhi-Ambedkar Divide: A Clash of Ideologies

One of the most profound contradictions in Gandhi's reformist efforts is his conflict with Dr. B.R. Ambedkar, a champion for the rights of Dalits and a leading figure in the fight against the caste system. While Gandhi fought for the upliftment of the "Harijans" (a term he coined for Dalits), Dr. Ambedkar believed that only radical social and political changes could eradicate the deeply entrenched caste system.

Gandhi's approach was one of gradual reform, focusing on integration and seeking a moral transformation of society. But Dr. Ambedkar, who was deeply disillusioned with the caste system, felt that true liberation for Dalits would only come through a complete abolition of the caste system and a rethinking of Hinduism itself. The two leaders disagreed sharply over issues like separate electorates for Dalits, with Gandhi even going on a fast unto death to oppose this. For Gandhi, unity was essential, but for Ambedkar, only the recognition of Dalits as separate, equal citizens could ensure their freedom.

This divide between Gandhi and Ambedkar is a testament to the conflicting ideas that shaped the Indian independence movement. Gandhi, despite his empathy for the oppressed, was unable to fully grasp the depth of the Dalits' suffering and their need for autonomy and dignity. On the other hand, Ambedkar's radical approach, though necessary for true social transformation, was seen by some as too divisive. Their disagreements reflect the tensions between reform within the existing system and the call for a complete dismantling of oppressive structures.

The Man Behind the Myth: Gandhi's Personal Life

In his personal life, Gandhi was a man of contradictions too. His experiments with celibacy, particularly living with young women to test his self-control, often raise eyebrows. He believed in the power of self-discipline, but these experiments, especially the way they were conducted, have been seen by some as deeply problematic. Gandhi's desire for purity in every aspect of life led him to push the boundaries of what was morally acceptable.

But perhaps it is this very complexity — this messiness of human existence — that makes Gandhi so relatable. After all, is it not through our contradictions that we grow? Isn't it in the moments of doubt, the moments when we question our own values, that we gain a deeper understanding of who we are?

A Final Thought: Gandhi's Legacy — Not Just a Story, But a Conversation

As I reflect on Gandhi's life, I'm reminded that reform is never clean or simple. It is often a messy, difficult process that asks us to hold conflicting truths at the same time. Gandhi's contradictions are part of his greatness. They show us that the pursuit of justice is not a straight path — it's winding, full of compromises and challenges, but also moments of profound clarity.

As we look back at his legacy, let's not just view him as a saint or a symbol of perfect morality. Let's see him as a man — a man who fought for freedom, equality, and justice, but who, like all of us, had to navigate the complex web of his own beliefs, doubts, and contradictions.

And maybe, just maybe, it's in those contradictions that the true lessons of Gandhi's life lie. Because in a world that often seems torn between extremes, perhaps it's our ability to hold these contradictions that makes us better, more empathetic human beings.

Periyar E.V. Ramasamy: The Crusader for Self-Respect

Some individuals are born into history, but Periyar E.V. Ramasamy wasn't just born into history—he made history. Periyar E.V. Ramasamy was the latter. He wasn't just a man; he was a rebellion, a storm that shattered centuries of oppression, blind faith, and social inequality. To simply call him a leader would be an understatement—he was **a force, a challenge, a revolution in human form**.

If there's one thing I have learned from Periyar, it is this: **self-respect is not a gift—it is taken, seized, and defended at all costs.**

I often wonder—what if Periyar had remained silent? What if he had never questioned the world around him? Would Tamil Nadu still be the land where people speak fearlessly, where rational thought is celebrated, where gods are not above scrutiny, and where equality is an expectation rather than an exception? His ideas didn't just shape a movement; they shaped **a state, a culture, a mindset.**

The Moment That Changed Everything

Periyar was born in 1879 into a wealthy, upper-caste family in Tamil Nadu. He could have lived comfortably, enjoying the privileges of his status. But he was not a man who could turn a blind eye to injustice. **He saw the chains of caste everywhere**, even in places that claimed to offer spiritual liberation.

It was his visit to Kashi, the sacred Hindu city, that **shattered his faith in religion forever**. There, he witnessed a brutal reality: Tamil-speaking devotees from "lower castes" were **denied water**—not because they were poor, not because they had sinned, but because they were born into the "wrong" caste. Their devotion meant nothing. Their prayers were irrelevant.

That was the moment he saw the truth—**religion, as practiced, was not about divinity but about control**. He didn't just leave the temple behind that day; he **walked out of an entire belief system** that justified inequality.

And once a mind is freed, it can never go back into its chains.

The Man Who Dared to Question Everything

Periyar didn't stop at criticizing caste. He **dared to question everything that enslaved human minds**—patriarchy, blind faith, language imposition, and even the very idea of god. **He didn't ask for reforms; he demanded a complete revolution.**

Through the **Self-Respect Movement**, he told people:

- **Don't bow to gods who keep you in chains.**
- **Don't follow customs that treat you as lesser.**
- **Don't accept that suffering in this life will reward you in the next.**
- **Demand respect. Demand dignity. Demand equality.**

His movement wasn't just about **destroying caste**—it was about **rebuilding human dignity** from the ground up. He encouraged inter-caste marriages, widow remarriages, and birth control at a time when even discussing women's rights was considered sinful.

He **fought not just for the oppressed but also for women**, believing that **a truly free society cannot exist without gender equality**. He declared that women had the right to choose their partners, to be educated, to work, and—most importantly—to have agency over their own lives.

The Battle of Ideologies: Periyar vs. Gandhi and Ambedkar

Periyar had his **sharpest ideological battles** with Gandhi and, to some extent, Ambedkar. While Gandhi **advocated for the upliftment of Dalits within Hinduism**, Periyar **wanted to annihilate the caste system altogether**. To him, reforming an oppressive system from within was futile—it had to be **burned down** so something better could take its place.

With Ambedkar, the difference was more nuanced. Both were **fierce warriors against caste oppression**, but their solutions differed. **Ambedkar turned to Buddhism, hoping to find liberation in a new spiritual path.** But Periyar? He **rejected all religion**. To him, the answer was not in replacing one god with another but in **rejecting god altogether**—because as long as people believed in divine authority, they would **remain vulnerable to human-made hierarchies**.

But despite these differences, their **ultimate goal was the same**—to **dismantle oppression and build a society where caste and hierarchy had no place.**

His Influence on Me

I don't just **respect** Periyar—I **carry his fire within me**. His words are not just history; they are **a living force** that shapes the way I see the world.

His **unapologetic rebellion**, his **refusal to conform**, and his **audacity to question what others accepted as fate**—that's what inspires me every day. He didn't just **fight for the oppressed**; he **handed them a weapon—the power of rationality, the courage of rebellion, and the conviction of self-respect**.

And that's what I take from him.

- **Never accept oppression as destiny.**
- **Never let tradition silence you.**
- **Never let fear decide your beliefs.**

Periyar's refusal to accept the status quo in his time resonates with me every day. He made me question my own complacency and taught me that real change begins when we challenge the very things we have accepted without question.

If Periyar has taught me anything, it is this: **to think, to challenge, and above all, to never bow down.**

Because **self-respect is not given. It is taken.**

The Legacy That Refuses to Die

Periyar may no longer be among us, but his fire has never died. His ideas are not relics of the past; they breathe through every fight for justice, every voice that refuses to be silenced, every act of defiance against oppression.

And perhaps nothing proves this more than the fact that even today, his name continues to stir controversy, resistance, and debate.

From political leaders vandalizing his statues to attempts to erase or vilify his legacy, there are forces that still fear the power of his ideas. They mock him, misinterpret him, and label him an extremist, not because he was wrong, but because his words still threaten the structures of power that thrive on caste, patriarchy, and blind faith.

It isn't surprising. Periyar never intended to be loved by the establishment—he intended to shake it to its core. And clearly, he still does.

Look around Tamil Nadu today—his influence is everywhere. In the rational debates, in the progressive policies, in the unapologetic demand for dignity. His movement was not just a political shift; it was a cultural awakening that still challenges outdated beliefs, still questions power, still refuses to bow.

But the question remains—are we ready to carry forward his legacy?

To truly honor Periyar is not to worship him, but to continue his fight. To think critically. To challenge authority. To stand against oppression—even when it's inconvenient, even when it's unpopular. Because if history has taught us anything, it is this:

Ideas don't die. Revolutions don't fade. And self-respect? Once awakened, it never bows again.

To truly honor Periyar is not just to remember him, but to embody his courage, his refusal to bow, and to carry his flame forward in every act of defiance against the status quo.

Jyotirao Phule and Savitribai Phule: Pioneers of Education and Equality

When we talk about **education** in the context of social transformation, there are few names that stand as tall as **Jyotirao Phule** and **Savitribai Phule**. You might think of them as just historical figures, but their journey isn't just about what they achieved—it's about **the relentless fight against a deeply ingrained social order** that sought to keep certain sections of society in the shadows of ignorance and inequality.

Imagine this: A young woman named **Savitribai Phule**, in 1848, stepping out into a world that wasn't ready for her. A world where **women's education** was unheard of, where **Dalits** were regarded as untouchables, not worthy of even the most basic rights. And yet, there she was, standing up for those who couldn't stand for themselves. She **opened the first school for girls** in Pune with her husband, **Jyotirao Phule**. It wasn't just an academic institution; it was a **revolutionary act**. Think about it—what kind of courage does it take to say, "We will create a future where knowledge isn't limited to a select few, but is available to all"?

Savitribai didn't just teach the girls who came to her school; she **became a symbol of defiance**. She faced **stone pelting**, verbal abuse, and social ostracization. People thought she was out of her mind. Yet, she continued to teach, to nurture the minds of young girls, believing that **education was the only way to lift the chains of oppression**. **She wasn't just an educator; she was a warrior**. Imagine her walking into the school every day with the weight of societal pressure on her shoulders, yet her eyes burning with hope for a better world. Her struggle wasn't easy, but she faced it head-on, **armed with nothing but her resolve and belief in the power of knowledge**.

And then there's **Jyotirao Phule**, the man who not only supported Savitribai but **laid the intellectual foundation** for this fight. He didn't just open schools; he **challenged the very idea** that certain groups of people—especially Dalits and women—didn't deserve education. Phule was deeply troubled by the hierarchical social system, which placed **Brahmins at the top** and systematically oppressed those at the bottom. His writings, particularly **"Gulamgiri"** (The Slavery), **shattered the comfortable narratives** that upheld caste-based discrimination. He didn't just speak against injustice; he **gave voice to the voiceless**, advocating for the **equality of all human beings**.

Here's a story that hits home for me: Imagine a young **Dalit child**, perhaps from a family that's never been allowed to enter a temple or drink water from the same well as the upper castes. This child, despite being born into a life of oppression, now has access to education, thanks to **Phule's radical vision**. That child isn't just learning to read and write; they're learning about their **dignity** and **worth**. That's what **Phule's education movement was all about**—it wasn't just about the curriculum, it was about **empowering people to challenge the system that kept them**

down. He knew that **knowledge is liberation**. He knew that **education could break the chains** of the caste system, and **he wasn't willing to let anyone be left behind**.

Phule's and Savitribai's schools were **more than places of learning**—they were **symbols of resistance**. They were places where **the marginalized were uplifted**, where **the oppressed were given tools to challenge the status quo**. Phule and Savitribai understood something that many still miss today: **Education is not just about gaining knowledge**. It's about **gaining the ability to change the world**. By opening schools for girls and Dalits, they not only defied tradition, but they **opened a door to a future where equality and justice were possible**.

But don't be fooled into thinking that it was all smooth sailing. Phule and Savitribai faced **relentless opposition**. Imagine the ridicule, the hatred, the stones thrown at Savitribai as she walked to school. **That was the cost of progress**. Their courage wasn't just in their actions, but in their **willingness to face adversity head-on**. Think about it—how many of us, in the face of such hostility, would have the courage to keep going? Yet, Phule and Savitribai did, because they knew that their work was **bigger than themselves**. It was about creating a future for generations to come.

The Legacy That Lives On

Today, as I look around, I see **their legacy in every classroom**, in every woman who is told she can't do something but then does it anyway, in every **Dalit student** who dares to walk into a university, in every **activist** who fights for the rights of the marginalized. Their struggle **wasn't just for education**, it was for **equality, dignity, and social justice**.

But here's the thing: Phule's vision is still **unfinished**. Yes, we've come a long way, but we are still fighting for **true equality**—whether it's in the classroom, the workplace, or society at large. **The caste system still casts its long shadow**, and **gender inequality** is still very much alive. Phule's call for a society where **no one is judged by their caste or gender** is **still relevant today**, maybe more than ever.

As we reflect on their contributions, I think it's important to ask ourselves: **Are we living up to their vision?** How far have we come in ensuring that **every child**, regardless of their caste or gender, has the right to an equal education and a life of dignity? We may not face the same social pressures that Phule and Savitribai did, but we are still faced with the **responsibility to continue their work**. We are the ones who must ask tough questions about the systems that still exclude and oppress.

Conclusion: The Unfinished Journey

Phule and Savitribai's fight was never just about education—it was about **empowerment**. It was about building a world where **everyone** has the chance to succeed, where **justice** and **equality** aren't just ideals, but **reality**. Their journey is far from over, and neither should ours be.

As I leave you with this, I want you to remember this: **Education is the gateway to change**, but **it's up to us to keep pushing the door open**. Jyotirao Phule and Savitribai Phule may have set the wheels in motion, but it's our generation that needs to ensure the engine keeps running.

The question is: **Are we ready to pick up where they left off?** The path to equality is **long**, but as Savitribai once said, **"The fight will be long, but it will be worth it"**.

Dravidian and Socialist Leaders: Shaping Modern Politics

I want to take you on a journey today—a journey into the heart of **Tamil Nadu's politics**, which is inextricably tied to the **Dravidian and socialist**

movements. If you look at the political landscape today, it's impossible to ignore the powerful influence of leaders like **C.N. Annadurai**, **M. Karunanidhi**, **K. Kamaraj**, and **Ram Manohar Lohia**. But here's the thing: their impact wasn't just political; it was **social**, **cultural**, and **transformative** in ways we often overlook.

C.N. Annadurai: The Voice of the Marginalized

Let's start with **C.N. Annadurai**, known affectionately as **Anna**. His name itself became a symbol of resistance. Imagine a time when **Tamil Nadu**, and much of India, was still dominated by a **Brahminical system**—a system that controlled knowledge, power, and resources. **Annadurai** came along with a fiery vision, one that rejected that structure altogether. He saw that **education, language, and self-respect** were keys to breaking free from this suffocating dominance.

What strikes me the most about **Anna** was his ability to **speak for the silenced**—for the communities that had long been excluded from the political narrative. He took **Periyar's rationalist ideology** and **amplified it**, turning it into a political force that **challenged the status quo**. **Annadurai didn't just talk about the need for change**—he was the **embodiment of that change**. His work laid the foundation for a society that demanded equality, not as a favor, but as a **fundamental right**.

His famous speeches were more than political rhetoric; they were **calls to action**. And the amazing thing about his leadership was that it resonated not just with the masses, but with those **who had been denied education**, those who had been told, **"You don't matter."**

M. Karunanidhi: The Architect of Change

Then, we have **M. Karunanidhi**, a man who **transformed the political narrative** in Tamil Nadu. You see, Karunanidhi wasn't just a politician;

he was a **visionary artist**. He understood the **power of media**—the power of **cinema**, **songs**, and **stories**—as tools for political change. I often think back to how **Karunanidhi's writings and films weren't just entertainment**. They were **battle cries**, urging the masses to rise against **social injustice**.

Karunanidhi inherited the mantle from **Annadurai**, but he took it to another level. He wasn't just content with **challenging the Brahminical order**; he sought to **reshape the very fabric of Tamil Nadu**. He embraced the ideals of **social welfare** and **affirmative action**, ensuring that **education and political representation** weren't privileges for the few, but **rights for all**.

And let's talk about **reservations**, an issue that's still so fiercely debated today. Karunanidhi was unwavering in his belief that **caste-based reservations were essential**. He didn't see them as a means to divide society; instead, he saw them as a **tool for empowerment**—a way to level the playing field for those who had been **historically deprived**.

K. Kamaraj: The Man of the People

K. Kamaraj, often regarded as the **"Kingmaker"** of Tamil Nadu, brought something else to the table: **practical solutions**. While **Annadurai and Karunanidhi** were revolutionaries in their own right, Kamaraj was the **man who built the foundation**. Kamaraj's focus was always on **grassroots development**, and he had an incredible understanding of **what the common people needed**.

One of the most remarkable things about him was his commitment to **education**. Under his leadership, Tamil Nadu became one of the first states to implement the **midday meal scheme**, which aimed to **provide nutritional support to children in schools**—a move that was nothing short of revolutionary at the time. It wasn't just about **feeding children**;

it was about ensuring **that every child had the chance to go to school**, regardless of their background.

What stands out for me is how Kamaraj balanced **visionary thinking with pragmatic policies**. He understood that **change had to come from the ground up**, and he worked tirelessly to **empower local communities**. Through his efforts, Tamil Nadu became a **model for welfare policies** that focused on **inclusivity**—because **for Kamaraj**, development wasn't about the elite; it was about the **people**.

Ram Manohar Lohia: The Socialist Firebrand

Let's now zoom out a little and look at the **larger socialist movement** in India. **Ram Manohar Lohia**, a towering figure in the Indian socialist movement, made a significant impact on caste-based reservations and the fight for **economic justice**. I can't help but think about how Lohia's insistence on **equity**—not just in education, but across all sectors—created a blueprint for policies that would later be implemented in the **Mandal Commission**.

Lohia's **passion for social justice** wasn't just academic; it was personal. He believed that the **backward classes**, the **Dalits**, and those left behind by India's **developmental narrative** needed to be uplifted not as a favor, but as a **duty**. His ideas set the stage for the **reservation system** that would later change the course of Indian politics. **The Mandal Commission**, which recommended reservations for **OBCs**, **relied heavily on Lohia's ideas**. His belief in **caste-based reservations** was not just a political stance but a deeply held **moral conviction**.

The Legacy: A Conversation with the Present

As I reflect on these leaders' contributions, I can't help but wonder—**how far have we come** since their time? Sure, we have affirmative action, we have political representation, and we have policies aimed at helping the marginalized. But when I look around, I still see deep divides—**the caste system, although outlawed, is still alive in many corners of our society**. The dream these leaders had of a truly **equal society** has not yet been fully realized.

But here's the thing—**their fight wasn't just about laws; it was about a vision**. A vision where people of all castes, all backgrounds, could stand side by side, not as equals in name, but as equals in reality. And while we may not be there yet, I believe their legacy lives on in the ongoing struggles of the marginalized—struggles for **education**, **representation**, and **justice**.

We may never know exactly how **Annadurai** or **Karunanidhi** would have tackled today's political climate, but one thing is clear: **their fight for justice wasn't about personal gain**—it was about lifting those who had been forgotten for so long. And that fight continues today.

They taught us that dignity is non-negotiable, and that any society worth building must be built on justice.

Global Revolution and Global Leaders: Shaping the World with Vision and Courage

As we look back at the leaders who shaped the course of **global history**, it's impossible to ignore the **revolutionaries** who fought for equality, justice, and the empowerment of the oppressed. These individuals weren't just confined to their nations; their **ideas** and **actions** created ripples that affected the world as a whole. They proved that **one person** could spark a change that would ignite revolutions across continents.

Nelson Mandela: The Face of Freedom

Let's begin with one of the most iconic figures in the global fight for **racial equality** and **human dignity**: **Nelson Mandela**. Imagine being imprisoned for **27 years**, not knowing if you'd ever see freedom again. But that was Mandela's reality, and yet, when he emerged from prison, he didn't seek vengeance. Instead, he sought **reconciliation**, uniting a **divided nation**.

What strikes me the most about **Mandela** was his ability to **transform personal suffering into collective healing**. His leadership wasn't just about his **time in prison**, though. It was about a **lifetime of resistance** against a brutal system that sought to oppress millions based on the color of their skin. His life's work became a symbol of **hope**, showing the world that **even in the face of grave injustice**, it is possible to emerge with **grace** and **integrity**.

Mandela's story isn't just about one man's struggle for freedom. It's about how **his resistance against apartheid became a global symbol**, a rallying cry for all oppressed people, not just in South Africa but in every corner of the globe.

Karl Marx: The Architect of Revolutionary Thought

When we talk about global revolutionaries, we cannot overlook **Karl Marx**, the philosopher whose ideas sparked some of the most significant political and social changes in the modern era. But here's the thing—Marx was more than just an economist or a philosopher. He was a **visionary** who sought to rewrite the rules of society, to change the entire fabric of the world in which we live. His ideas weren't just theories on paper; they became the **blueprint** for **revolutionary movements** that reshaped entire nations.

Now, Marx's **philosophical revolution** began with a single, bold idea: the **critique of capitalism**. He believed that capitalism, as an economic system, inherently led to **exploitation**—the rich, owning the means of production, while the poor, the workers, were exploited for their labor. **Marx argued** that the relationship between the two classes—**capitalists** and **workers**—was inherently unequal and that this inequality would eventually lead to **revolution**. His famous phrase, **"Workers of the world, unite!"**, became a rallying cry for **working-class liberation** around the globe.

But let me take a step back. We have to understand Marx's deeper impact. You see, Marx wasn't just writing about economics in a vacuum; he was writing with a **vision of humanity's future**—a future where **class distinctions** were erased and people lived in harmony, based on equality and mutual respect. Marx's ultimate goal was the **establishment of a classless society**, where the state would no longer serve the interests of the wealthy elite, but the **collective good of all people**.

The Communist Manifesto: A Call to Action

If we look at one of Marx's most important works, the **Communist Manifesto**, written in collaboration with Friedrich Engels in 1848, we see a document that was as much about **theoretical critique** as it was a **call to action**. The manifesto wasn't a gentle suggestion; it was a **radical declaration** that aimed to rattle the very foundations of **capitalist society**.

I remember reading it for the first time and being struck by its urgency. Marx and Engels didn't just want to critique society—they wanted to **transform it**, to tear down the structures of power that kept millions in **poverty** and **subjugation**. The manifesto's concluding words, **"Workers of the world, unite! You have nothing to lose but your chains"**, have echoed across every revolution since.

The thing about **Marxism** that often gets lost is its **emphasis on human dignity**. Marx's **vision wasn't about creating a utopia for the elite or the powerful**, it was about creating a world where the **working class**—the people who had been marginalized for centuries—could finally stand on **equal footing**. It's a vision that continues to resonate today, especially as we see increasing inequality in our globalized world.

The Legacy of Marx: From Russia to China

Marx's ideas didn't just remain in the realm of academia or political theory. His thoughts inspired some of the most **dramatic revolutions in history**, starting with the **Russian Revolution of 1917**, where **Vladimir Lenin** took Marx's ideas and applied them to the **Russian context**. Lenin's success in overthrowing the Tsarist regime and establishing the **Soviet Union** was a direct outcome of Marx's revolutionary theory.

But it didn't stop there. **Mao Zedong** took Marxist-Leninist ideology and adapted it to the Chinese context, resulting in the **Chinese Communist Revolution**. **Cuba's Fidel Castro** also drew heavily on Marx's ideas, shaping a new political order based on the equality and redistribution of wealth.

However, Marx's legacy isn't without controversy. While his ideas of class struggle inspired revolutions, the ways in which they were implemented—often through authoritarian regimes—have been heavily debated. The failure of many Marxist regimes to establish true **democracy** or a **classless society** has led to critiques of Marxism's applicability in the real world. And yet, we can't ignore how Marx's critique of capitalism continues to shape **modern political discourse**, especially in today's global debates over inequality, wealth distribution, and **workers' rights**.

The Relevance of Marx Today

So, where do we stand today in relation to **Karl Marx's ideas**? Despite the decline of Marxist regimes in the 20th century, his critique of capitalism is more relevant than ever. The issue of **income inequality** has skyrocketed in the past few decades, and **working-class movements** are seeing a resurgence, with people demanding **higher wages**, **better working conditions**, and **greater wealth redistribution**.

Marx's ideas about the **alienation of labor** also feel incredibly **timely**. The **gig economy** and **automation** have further distanced workers from the products of their labor, and many people today are experiencing the very sense of **alienation** that Marx warned about. He predicted that in a capitalist society, workers would lose their connection to the work they do, becoming mere **cogs in a machine**. In many ways, we can see this happening in **today's workforce**.

The rise of **corporations**, the **financialization of the economy**, and the **globalization of labor** all echo Marx's warnings about the **concentration of wealth and power** in the hands of a few. **Capitalism**, for all its promises of growth and prosperity, has once again failed to deliver a fair system, as **billionaire wealth** continues to grow while millions of people around the world struggle to make ends meet.

Marx's Enduring Influence

So, what do we take from all of this? **Karl Marx wasn't just a theorist**; he was a **revolutionary** who shaped global politics in ways we still feel today. His critique of capitalism, his advocacy for workers, and his belief in **human emancipation** still resonate deeply in today's world. Whether we agree with every aspect of Marx's theories or not, there is no denying that he sparked a conversation that has led to profound **political movements**, **economic theories**, and **revolutions** throughout the last century.

What Marx truly did was **challenge the status quo**, forcing the world to confront uncomfortable truths about **economic inequality** and **social justice**. And in that, his legacy lives on—shaping modern political ideologies and movements, and urging us to ask the tough questions about the kind of world we want to build.

Che Guevara: The Revolutionary Heartbeat of Resistance

When we speak of revolutionaries who were willing to sacrifice everything for their cause, **Ernesto "Che" Guevara** stands tall. A man whose life was driven by a relentless pursuit of justice, Che's journey from a **medical student** to a **guerrilla leader** is nothing short of remarkable. But what makes Che particularly inspiring is not just his military prowess or his involvement in the Cuban Revolution. It's his **unwavering belief in the necessity of challenging injustice**—the kind of injustice that doesn't just hurt individuals but **entrenches systems of inequality** that keep the poor, the marginalized, and the oppressed trapped in cycles of suffering.

Che once said, **"If you tremble with indignation at every injustice, then you are a comrade of mine."** This quote isn't just a rallying cry for revolutionaries; it's an invitation. It speaks to all of us who **cannot stand by** when we witness inequality or oppression. It's an invitation to join the fight—not just for **political freedom**, but for **human dignity** and **social equity**.

Imagine standing in the face of injustice, seeing the suffering of countless people, and realizing you cannot stay silent. **Che Guevara didn't just stand against injustice**—he actively **challenged it**, even at great personal cost. For him, **silence in the face of injustice** was a betrayal of everything worth fighting for. This is what made him a revolutionary not just in the political sense, but in a deeply moral one. His actions were born from a place of compassion, a refusal to accept a world where people could live in **oppression** just because of where they were born or what system they were caught up in.

The Ideals and the Reality of the Revolution

We often talk about **Che Guevara's revolution** as if it were an isolated event, tied to the **Cuban revolution** or his later guerrilla movements in **Bolivia**. But in reality, Che's revolution was **global**. It was a fight against the imperialist forces that crushed the lives of people in Latin America, Africa, and beyond. Che's dream was of a world **where justice prevailed over greed**, where the poor could rise above the systems that kept them down.

But the path of revolution is not without its complexities. Che's vision was always about **people's liberation**, but in practice, his methods often led to deep and difficult contradictions. The **Cuban Revolution**, for example, while providing hope and a sense of freedom to many in Cuba, also came with sacrifices. **Che's methods** were sometimes harsh, and in his pursuit of social justice, he didn't shy away from violence if he believed it was necessary to achieve the revolution's goals.

It's here that the **complexity of Che's legacy** begins to show itself. He wasn't a perfect man, and his beliefs evolved in ways that forced him to confront the realities of revolutionary politics. Yet, in his heart, Che remained steadfast: the **oppressor had to be overthrown**, and the **poor and oppressed** had to be liberated at any cost.

Che Guevara's Global Impact

The significance of Che's life isn't confined to Cuba or Latin America. His influence reached across the globe, touching the hearts and minds of those who, like him, could not sit idly by while the powerful and the wealthy trampled on the less fortunate.

Let me tell you a story I find particularly inspiring: In the 1960s, when **Che was in Africa**, he saw firsthand the devastating effects of colonialism and imperialism on African nations. In places like **Algeria** and **Congo**, Che's ideals resonated with local revolutionaries who were fighting against their colonial masters. Even as he struggled in his efforts to start a successful insurgency in the Congo, his message remained clear: **every act of resistance matters**. **Che didn't just see the fight against imperialism as a regional struggle**, he saw it as **a global mission**. Whether it was in Latin America, Africa, or Asia, he believed the struggle for justice was one that **united oppressed peoples everywhere**.

Even today, the image of **Che Guevara**, with his **beret and intense gaze**, stands as a symbol of resistance. Whether we agree with all of his actions or not, what is undeniable is the fact that Che became a **global icon of defiance**—a figure who inspired countless movements against injustice. **In that sense**, the revolutionary Che Guevara has transcended history, continuing to inspire **activists, freedom fighters**, and **social justice warriors** who refuse to stand idle when they see injustice.

Che's Legacy in Today's World

In today's world, we still face the same injustices Che fought against. From **economic inequality** to **political oppression**, the issues Che confronted are still very much alive. And here's where his message still holds weight: if you are the kind of person who **trembles with indignation** when you see oppression, then you are not alone. You're part of a **legacy**—one that extends beyond Che himself. You are part of the ongoing struggle for a world where justice isn't just a lofty ideal, but a lived reality.

Che Guevara's **legacy isn't just about the politics of revolution**, but about the very **ethics of resistance**. His words echo in the hearts of those who **stand against injustice**, wherever it may appear. His story reminds us that **change** doesn't come easily, but that **every action against**

oppression—no matter how small—**counts**. And maybe, just maybe, we should all take a little of Che's revolutionary spirit with us, as we continue to fight for a fairer, more just world.

The Legacy of Global Revolutionaries

As we reflect on the lives and ideologies of global leaders like **Che Guevara**, **Karl Marx**, and others who dedicated their lives to the struggle for justice and equality, we are reminded of the transformative power of **revolutionary thought**. These figures weren't just dreamers; they were **doers**, willing to take action, challenge the status quo, and confront the deeply entrenched systems of oppression.

The **influence of their ideas** continues to echo through the corridors of history, shaping modern political discourse and inspiring countless movements for **social change** across the globe. They saw injustice not as an unfortunate reality but as a call to action. Their commitment to **empowering the oppressed**, whether through **revolution**, **ideological struggle**, or **grassroots activism**, has created a ripple effect that still impacts societies today.

But we must also remember the complexity of their legacies. **Revolutionary movements**, though driven by high ideals, are often marked by contradictions and struggles in implementation. The balance between **theoretical purity** and **practical reality** is not easy to achieve, and as we look at their histories, we must learn from both their **achievements and mistakes**.

Yet, their **core message remains timeless**: the fight for justice, equality, and freedom is **endless**. It is a struggle that transcends borders, eras, and ideologies. And while their methods may have been controversial or their results mixed, the essential truth is that they **shaped the world in profound ways**, urging us to never settle for a world where injustice reigns.

As we navigate the complex and often tumultuous landscape of our own time, let us remember the legacies of these leaders. **Their lives remind us that the fight for a better world is ongoing**, that we must always stand against inequality, and that **revolution—whether in thought or action—is the power to change everything**.

It's up to us now to carry the torch, to ensure that their dreams are not forgotten, but instead **transformed into the ongoing reality of a more just and compassionate world**.

The Mandal Era and Beyond: The Politics of Reservation

The **Mandal Commission's recommendations**, implemented in 1990 under the leadership of **V.P. Singh**, became a watershed moment in India's political history, fundamentally altering the landscape of **caste-based politics**. The decision to extend **reservation** benefits to the **Other Backward Classes (OBCs)** in government jobs and educational institutions ignited a wave of political and social mobilization, changing the course of Indian democracy.

For centuries, caste had been the dominant axis of inequality in Indian society, with **OBCs**, along with **Scheduled Castes (SCs)** and **Scheduled Tribes (STs)**, bearing the brunt of **social, economic, and educational marginalization**. The Mandal Commission was tasked with investigating the socio-economic conditions of the **OBCs**, and its report, which recommended affirmative action in the form of **reservation**, was a landmark attempt to address systemic disparities. However, the road to implementing the Mandal recommendations was neither smooth nor devoid of controversy.

The announcement in **1990** that the government would implement the Mandal Commission's **recommendations** sparked a nationwide **debate**.

Protests erupted across the country, particularly in the urban, **upper-caste** segments, with many seeing it as an infringement on their rights to access government positions and education. The **backlash** was fierce, with widespread **student protests** in cities like Delhi, Mumbai, and Varanasi, most notably led by those who felt the **caste-based quotas** would compromise their opportunities.

On the other hand, the decision was hailed as a **revolutionary step** by **OBCs**, who had long been deprived of opportunities despite making up a significant portion of India's population. It gave birth to a new **political consciousness** among these communities, who began to see themselves as a **unified political force** capable of shaping the nation's future. The **Mandal Era** thus laid the foundation for a **new political landscape**, one where **caste-based identity politics** became central to the aspirations of millions.

The Rise of Regional Powerhouses

The implementation of the Mandal recommendations also led to the rise of **regional political leaders** who capitalized on the **mobilization of OBCs**. Leaders like **Lalu Prasad Yadav**, **Mulayam Singh Yadav**, and **Mayawati** emerged as champions of **OBC, Dalit, and backward caste communities**.

- **Lalu Prasad Yadav**, a charismatic leader from Bihar, was one of the first to skillfully harness the **political potential** of OBCs. His victory in the **Bihar Legislative Assembly elections** in 1990, riding on the back of the Mandal Commission's implementation, transformed him into a significant political figure. Yadav's focus on **inclusive governance** and his strong stance against the perceived dominance of upper castes in the state's politics allowed him to build a **massive support base** among OBCs and Dalits. His leadership marked the beginning of the **"Mandalisation"** of Indian politics, where **caste** became a central theme in the rise of political leaders.

- Similarly, **Mulayam Singh Yadav** in Uttar Pradesh, a state that has always been at the heart of **caste-based politics**, capitalized on the OBC mobilization to become a formidable political force. His leadership of the **Samajwadi Party** and his policy focus on **empowering backward classes** made him a key player in the state's politics, challenging the dominance of **Brahminical elites**. Mulayam's success lay in his ability to **balance caste-based politics** with the demand for **social justice**.
- In the same vein, **Mayawati**, leader of the **Bahujan Samaj Party (BSP)**, took the **Dalit empowerment** agenda to new heights. Her rise to power as the Chief Minister of Uttar Pradesh in 1995, as a Dalit woman, symbolized the potential of caste-based politics in creating **alternative power structures**. Mayawati's BSP became a formidable force in the state, articulating the aspirations of Dalits, backward classes, and the marginalized communities. Her **social engineering** strategies, which brought together Dalits, OBCs, and even upper-caste factions in her coalition, were a direct result of the Mandal Commission's political ramifications.

The Politics of Reservation: Challenges and Controversies

While the Mandal Commission's recommendations paved the way for **increased political representation** and social mobility for **OBCs**, the politics of **reservation** has not been without its share of controversy and debate. Over time, the reservation system expanded to include **economically weaker sections (EWS)**, and debates about its **impact on meritocracy** have been at the forefront of public discussions.

Critics argue that reservation has, at times, **undermined merit-based selections** in education and government jobs. They suggest that the system has not led to an **overall improvement** in the socio-economic conditions of the beneficiaries, pointing to issues such as **poor implementation**, **corruption**, and the **creeping politicization** of the reservation system. Furthermore, there are ongoing concerns about the **"creamy layer"** within the OBCs, leading to a **misallocation of resources** and continued **inequality** within backward classes themselves.

However, supporters of reservation maintain that while the system is **imperfect**, it has been instrumental in **creating opportunities** for millions who were historically excluded from educational and professional fields. They argue that the reservation system is not just a mechanism for **affirmative action**, but a **tool for social justice** in a deeply unequal society. Without it, many argue, India would have continued to **perpetuate systemic discrimination** against lower-caste and backward communities.

The Mandal Era's Legacy: A Political and Social Transformation

The **Mandal Era** marked the beginning of a new **political order** in India, one in which caste-based politics became inextricably linked with **regional power** and **social justice movements**. It led to the **empowerment of marginalized communities**, particularly the **OBCs**, and redefined the electoral landscape of states like Bihar, Uttar Pradesh, and Tamil Nadu.

While it brought some much-needed political recognition to communities that had long been ignored, the era also highlighted the **deep divisions** within Indian society, particularly in terms of **caste**, **class**, and **region**. The rise of caste-based political parties and the growing importance of identity politics has, however, led to a certain **fragmentation** of India's political space, making coalition politics a more complex and often unpredictable venture.

The **Mandal Commission's legacy** is a double-edged sword—it has brought **representation** and **empowerment**, but it has also sparked

controversy and debate about **affirmative action**, **merit**, and **social equality**. As we move forward, it is clear that the politics of **reservation** will continue to be a defining factor in Indian politics, shaping both policy and identity in profound ways.

The Mandal Era and its aftermath have not just reshaped political alliances but have also sparked a **continuing conversation** about how India can build a more **inclusive** and **just society**, one that **celebrates diversity** while addressing the deep-rooted **inequalities** that continue to affect millions.

Dalit-Bahujan Politics in the 21st Century

In the **21st century**, the **Dalit-Bahujan** politics in India has taken on a new **dimension**, shaped by the emergence of **new leaders** and the continuing struggles of historically oppressed communities. Among the most notable figures in this new political landscape is **Mayawati**, who not only became the first **Dalit woman** to hold the position of **Chief Minister of Uttar Pradesh**, but also became a symbol of empowerment for millions who were once relegated to the margins of Indian society.

The **rise of Dalit-Bahujan leaders** like Mayawati, **Lalu Prasad Yadav**, **Mulayam Singh Yadav**, and **K. Chandrashekar Rao** has been a testament to the ongoing battle for **representation**, **empowerment**, and **social justice**. These leaders have built political platforms around the **assertion of caste identities** and the promise of **equity** for the **marginalized communities** in India. They have used caste-based politics as a **vehicle for social change**, challenging the traditional Brahminical dominance in the country's **political sphere**.

Mayawati's **political career** is particularly significant. As the **leader of the Bahujan Samaj Party (BSP)**, she not only focused on Dalit upliftment but also managed to build a **coalition** of Dalits, OBCs, and even some **upper-caste** groups, making her a formidable political figure in **Uttar**

Pradesh. Her **rise to power** marked a **new chapter in Dalit-Bahujan politics**, showing that communities that were once politically invisible could rise to the highest echelons of power. Her tenure as the **Chief Minister** was marked by her **commitment** to creating a **symbolic and political space** for Dalits in the state's power structures, along with her emphasis on **infrastructure development** and **welfare schemes** for the poor.

However, despite the **advancements** made by leaders like Mayawati, the **struggle for Dalit-Bahujan empowerment** is far from over. The **persistent inequalities** of caste continue to affect large sections of Indian society, especially in rural areas. While **reservation policies** have provided some relief, they have not **eradicated caste-based discrimination** or **economic disparity**. The **Brahminical elite** still holds considerable power in many sectors, including **politics**, **education**, and **the economy**, which often limits the scope of policy reforms that could bring about true social change.

The Changing Dynamics of Dalit-Bahujan Politics

Dalit-Bahujan politics is also undergoing a shift in the **current century**. While **caste-based mobilization** continues to be a driving force, there is also a growing recognition that **economic justice** is just as important as **political representation**. Leaders like **Kanshi Ram**, **Mayawati**, and **Mulayam Singh Yadav** understood that **empowerment** comes not just from political power but also from **educational reforms**, **economic development**, and **social reforms**. Their agendas focused on giving Dalits and Bahujans the **tools** to break the shackles of their caste-based oppression by providing them **access to education**, **employment opportunities**, and **social security**.

This new focus on **economic empowerment** has led to more **inclusive policies**, such as **reservation quotas**, aimed at addressing the needs of **marginalized groups**. However, the **implementation** of these policies remains uneven. Many Dalits, despite enjoying reservations in government jobs and educational institutions, still face **systemic discrimination** in **public spaces** and **social interactions**. In rural India, the **untouchability practices** and **caste-based violence** continue to persist, requiring a comprehensive approach to social reform, which includes **economic opportunities**, **legal protection**, and a **change in cultural attitudes**.

The emergence of **new political parties** like the **Aam Aadmi Party** (AAP) and the **Indian National Congress**'s increasing emphasis on **inclusive politics** has also added complexity to the Dalit-Bahujan political scene. The dynamics between these traditional parties and the newer ones will likely continue to evolve, particularly as **youth movements** and **new generations of Dalit-Bahujan leaders** push for **greater representation** and **policy reforms**.

Challenges to Dalit-Bahujan Politics

Despite the remarkable strides made in Dalit-Bahujan politics, **challenges** remain. One of the key obstacles to further **empowerment** is the continued **caste-based violence** that plagues many parts of India. Even with constitutional safeguards like the **Scheduled Castes and Scheduled Tribes (Prevention of Atrocities) Act** in place, **Dalit atrocities** remain prevalent, especially in rural areas. **Honor killings**, **discriminatory practices** in **villages**, and **limited access to resources** are daily realities for many from these communities.

Moreover, the politics of **reservation** continues to be a contentious issue. Critics argue that **reservation policies**, while well-intentioned, have led to **unintended consequences** like **reverse discrimination** and **merit-based exclusions**. However, **supporters** of these policies assert that

reservation remains necessary to **level the playing field** and provide equal opportunities for historically marginalized communities.

Another challenge lies in the **fragmentation** of the Dalit-Bahujan vote. While parties like **BSP** and **RJD** have traditionally been strong advocates for these communities, **internal divisions** and **personal rivalries** within these parties often undermine their collective strength. The rise of **regional parties**, which focus on specific caste or religious identities, further complicates the unity of the Dalit-Bahujan block, making it difficult for them to form a cohesive political front.

The Road Ahead

Looking ahead, **Dalit-Bahujan politics** will continue to evolve, but its ultimate success will depend on how well it addresses the **multiple facets** of **oppression** that these communities face. **Political representation**, **educational access**, and **economic opportunities** must be integrated into a **holistic approach** to **social justice**. It is essential to ensure that **caste-based discrimination** and **caste-based violence** are eradicated through **stronger legal frameworks** and **enforced social policies**.

The rise of **young Dalit-Bahujan leaders** who are more attuned to the **economic realities** of the 21st century, combined with the persistence of **activists and academics** fighting for **social change**, gives hope that the battle for equality is far from over. There is a growing recognition that **empowerment** is not just about **political representation** but also about **changing the social and economic fabric** of Indian society.

In conclusion, **Dalit-Bahujan politics** in the 21st century is a **continuing struggle**, one that reflects the **resilience** of communities that have fought for centuries to assert their rights, dignity, and identity. The **next phase** of this struggle will be defined by how well these communities can **synthesize political action** with **social and economic reforms** that bring about **lasting change**. The journey is far from over, but it is a journey that continues to shape India's evolving democracy.

The legacy of the Mandal Era extends far beyond policy—it redefined the contours of political representation and gave voice to communities historically pushed to the margins. While caste remains a deeply entrenched factor in Indian society, the post-Mandal political landscape ushered in a more inclusive and assertive democracy. It prompted the mainstreaming of backward class interests, challenged upper-caste dominance, and led to the rise of coalition politics centered on identity and justice. As India continues to grapple with the dual challenges of equity and merit, the Mandal moment stands as a reminder that affirmative action is not merely about redressal but about restructuring access to power. The road ahead demands both introspection and innovation—ensuring that the principles of social justice evolve with the needs of a changing nation.

Charting the Path to an Equal Society

The journey of caste-based politics in India has been shaped by a series of **visionary leaders**, each contributing in unique ways to the ongoing struggle for **social justice**, **equality**, and **representation**. Their roles, while diverse, have always been driven by a common goal: to **challenge caste-based discrimination** and create a more **equitable society**.

Some leaders, like **Mahatma Gandhi**, sought **reform within the existing social structures**, using non-violence and dialogue to encourage change from within the system. Others, such as **Dr. B.R. Ambedkar**, took a more radical approach, pushing for the complete **restructuring** of India's social, political, and economic systems to dismantle the entrenched caste hierarchies. **Periyar**, **Jyotirao Phule**, and the leaders of the **Dravidian movement** believed in **rationalism, self-respect, and social equality**, challenging not just the political system, but also the deep-rooted cultural and religious norms that perpetuated caste-based oppression.

The **legacy** of these leaders, both reformist and revolutionary, continues to resonate in the political and social spheres of modern India. Their ideologies have laid the **foundation for policies of affirmative action**, **reservation**, and **welfare programs**, though much work remains to be done. The ongoing struggle for **Dalit and Bahujan rights**, the **empowerment of women**, and the **eradication of caste-based violence** are issues that continue to define contemporary political discourse.

The caste-based politics that emerged in the wake of these movements is a **dynamic force** that has transformed India's social landscape. While the path to **true equality** is long and fraught with challenges, the journey itself reflects the **resilience** and **resolve** of the marginalized. As we continue to witness the rise of new leaders and movements advocating for justice and representation, the foundational work laid by these trailblazers remains an essential touchstone for **social change**.

In the end, the struggle for a **caste-free India** is far from over. It requires not just political and social reforms but a deep-rooted change in how we, as a society, view identity, power, and justice. The legacy of these leaders continues to guide and inspire us, reminding us that the fight for **equality** and **justice** is ongoing and must be **fought with conviction, unity, and purpose**.

CASTE AND ELECTORAL POLITICS

> *"In the theatre of democracy, caste is not merely a backstage identity — it is often the script, the spotlight, and the stage itself".*

Caste and politics have historically intersected and continue to do so in the present political landscape of India. The relationship between caste and politics has been evolving, but caste remains a powerful force influencing electoral strategies, party dynamics, and governance structures.

Why does caste continue to dominate Indian politics? We have a fundamental understanding of democracy, and we know that caste should not be the foundation of political decisions. So why does it still shape the political narrative so strongly? In a democratic system that claims to uphold equality, it is unsettling that caste remains a key factor in governance, elections, and representation. Shouldn't political decisions be driven by the values of justice, equality, and the true needs of the people, rather than the deep-seated divisions of caste? It's time to question why caste still holds such power in a system that is supposed to guarantee fairness and opportunity for all.

To better understand this, we can look at it as a story — one that reveals the deep-rooted influence of caste in Indian politics and society.

Imagine a society that strives for fairness, equality, and the common good — a society that promises that every citizen, regardless of their background, has an equal opportunity to thrive. This is the essence of democracy, a system built on the foundation of justice. However, in this story, there is a shadow that refuses to fade: caste.

This shadow first began during the colonial era when the British divided people into groups based on caste, creating divisions that would serve their rule. When India gained independence, the new Constitution aimed to bring about equality and social justice, offering protections for those historically oppressed by caste. But despite these efforts, the system has never fully shed the weight of caste.

As time has passed, caste has continued to play a role in Indian politics, often more prominently than one would expect in a democratic system. Political parties, to gain votes, cater to specific caste groups, reinforcing these identities rather than focusing on broader issues like economic development or social welfare. In many parts of the country, a person's caste still plays a major role in determining their access to power, opportunities, and even basic rights.

Now, as the story unfolds in modern India, the question arises: Why does caste still hold such sway over the political process? Shouldn't politics be about addressing the actual needs of the people — ensuring justice, equality, and opportunity for all? Instead, caste continues to divide and define, standing in the way of the true spirit of democracy.

This is the struggle of the story — a society striving for progress, yet hindered by its past, where the shackles of caste remain firmly in place. The question now is whether India can break free from these divisions and move toward a future where politics is truly about people, not about the labels society has placed upon them.

A Political Journey with cast

The past and history are fundamental to understanding any subject, and this is no exception. To truly grasp the significance of caste in politics, one must first delve into its historical roots and evolution. Without acknowledging the history, we cannot fully comprehend the present dynamics or the impact caste continues to have in Indian politics.

Caste has profoundly shaped India's social and political framework for centuries, long before colonial rule. Under the traditional caste system, social and economic roles were determined by caste, creating rigid divisions that extended deeply into politics. These divisions weren't just a matter of social structure—they were also about power and access, where political representation and decision-making were largely controlled by upper-caste elites.

During British colonial rule, these caste divisions were not only preserved but were actively institutionalized by the colonial government to maintain control over India's vast and diverse population. The British recognized the utility of these divisions and used them to their advantage, introducing policies that solidified caste-based identities in the political sphere. One of the key measures was the **Morley-Minto Reforms of 1909**, which introduced separate electorates, allowing different caste and religious groups to elect their own representatives. This policy didn't just acknowledge caste—it capitalized on it, creating an electoral system where identity was defined by caste rather than national unity.

The **Communal Award of 1932** went even further, extending separate electorates not only to Muslims but also to Sikhs, Christians, and the **depressed classes** (Scheduled Castes). This move entrenched caste in India's political structure, ensuring that political representation became a reflection of caste identities rather than a unified national vision. The introduction of separate electorates set the stage for a political landscape in which caste-based loyalty and representation became the norm.

Dr. **B.R. Ambedkar** is, of course, a central figure in this context. His role in the fight against caste-based oppression is well-established, and we have already explored his contributions in earlier chapters. However, what's crucial here is his understanding of the political implications of caste. Dr. Ambedkar's advocacy for the **Scheduled Castes** led to the establishment of **affirmative action policies** in independent India, which were designed to counterbalance the historical injustice faced by marginalized groups. Through reservations in education, employment, and political representation, these policies aimed to provide equal opportunities and representation to those who had been systematically excluded.

Despite these efforts, the political system continued to function within a caste-conscious framework. Political parties, whether at the national or regional level, continued to align themselves with specific caste groups, forming alliances that would guarantee electoral success. This gave rise to caste-based political parties, caste became the cornerstone of political mobilization, and parties recognized the power of caste-based vote banks.

The historical context of caste in politics provides crucial insights into why caste remains a dominant force in India's democracy today. From the **Morley-Minto Reforms** to the **Communal Award**, and the rise of caste-based parties, caste has been woven into the fabric of Indian political life. While India has made strides toward social justice and equality, the legacies of caste-based political representation continue to shape how candidates are selected, how voters align with parties, and how coalitions are built.

In the end, understanding this history isn't just about looking back at the colonial period or Dr. Ambedkar's struggles. It's about seeing how these historical events continue to influence the political dynamics of modern

India. The story of caste in politics is a complex one, and it's clear that its impact is far from over.

Caste and Political Parties

Politics and caste in India are not just intersecting lines—they are tangled threads woven so deeply into the fabric of governance that one cannot be understood without the other. The political map of India has long been painted in the colors of caste identities, shaping the rise and fall of leaders, the formation of governments, and the very aspirations of the electorate.

Emergence of Caste-Based Political Parties

Caste has always been a marker of identity, but its transformation into a political force began in earnest during the late colonial and early post-independence period. As democracy took root, caste groups realized that electoral power could be wielded as effectively as social hierarchy had been in the past. What followed was a calculated mobilization—caste communities started aligning themselves with parties that promised them representation, protection, and privileges.

Regional caste-based parties, such as the Bahujan Samaj Party (BSP) in Uttar Pradesh, emerged as powerful forces advocating for Dalit rights. Similarly, parties in Tamil Nadu, like the Dravidar Kazhagam and its offshoots, sought to dismantle Brahminical dominance, giving birth to the powerful Dravidian movement. These parties did not emerge in a vacuum—they were the result of decades, if not centuries, of social struggles.

Imagine a young Dalit man in the 1950s, standing outside a polling booth, hesitant but hopeful. His father never had a say in who governed the land, and his grandfather was told he didn't even belong in the same village as those in power. But now, he casts his vote for a party that speaks his language, represents his struggles, and promises him dignity. That is the power of caste-based politics—it has given voice to the historically voiceless, even if at times it has also perpetuated divisions.

Role of Dominant Castes in National and Regional Parties

While caste-based parties emerged to challenge the status quo, dominant caste groups have never loosened their grip on power. National parties, whether it be the Congress in the early years or the Bharatiya Janata Party (BJP) today, have long understood that electoral success depends on caste equations. Their leadership, their candidate selection, and even their grassroots networks are deeply tied to dominant caste interests.

Take, for example, the role of the Yadavs in Uttar Pradesh and Bihar. These states have seen the rise of strong political figures from the Yadav community, such as Mulayam Singh Yadav and Lalu Prasad Yadav, who consolidated their caste groups into formidable vote banks. Meanwhile, in Maharashtra, the Marathas have exerted an undeniable influence over politics, ensuring that their interests remain at the forefront of governance.

The regional parties, too, have followed similar patterns. In Tamil Nadu, Thevars, Vanniyars, and Gounders have historically aligned with different Dravidian parties, ensuring that their dominance is maintained. The same is true for Jats in Haryana and Rajasthan, and Patels in Gujarat. These dominant caste groups have used their numerical strength and historical privileges to negotiate political power, often sidelining smaller and less organized caste communities.

Party Strategies: Caste-Based Ticket Distribution and Alliances

Political parties do not operate in a vacuum; they strategize, calculate, and maneuver based on caste realities. Every election season, candidate lists are carefully curated based on caste demographics. The process is not about merit or vision—it is a numbers game.

If a constituency has a majority of a particular caste group, parties ensure that their candidate belongs to that caste. If no single caste dominates, alliances are formed—parties bring together different caste groups under a common electoral umbrella, often by making promises of reservations, welfare schemes, and even symbolic gestures like temple visits and community events.

But what does this mean for the common voter? Imagine an election rally where a leader passionately declares that his party will fight for the upliftment of a particular caste. The crowd cheers. But is this really about empowerment, or is it just another way of securing votes? The harsh truth is that while caste-based politics has provided representation to marginalized groups, it has also reduced democracy to a game of identities rather than ideas.

Caste and political parties in India are inseparable, and the reality is far more complex than a simple story of oppression and empowerment. While caste-based politics has given marginalized groups a seat at the table, it has also reinforced the very divisions that democracy sought to erase. The real question remains—can Indian politics move beyond caste, or will it continue to be the defining factor of electoral success? Only time will tell, but for now, caste remains the silent, yet loud, player in the grand theatre of Indian democracy.

Electoral Trends and Voter Behavior

Politics in India is shaped by a multitude of factors—economic policies, leadership charisma, development agendas, and identity-based considerations, among others. Among these, caste remains an undeniable force, but it is not the sole determinant of voter behavior. Elections are often a complex interplay of aspirations, governance records, ideological leanings, and social identities. While caste plays a role in mobilization and representation, it is crucial to recognize that Indian elections are also influenced by larger socio-political narratives that transcend identity politics.

Electoral Patterns in Lok Sabha and State Assembly Elections

Imagine stepping into a political war room during election season. You might expect to see discussions about economic policies, education reforms, or international relations. Instead, you'll find analysts breaking down vote banks, calculating caste compositions, and predicting shifts in alliances. Elections in India are rarely just about performance or vision; they are a delicate balancing act of multiple factors, including governance, alliances, and identity-based mobilization.

This isn't a new phenomenon. From the first general elections in 1952 to the present day, various factors, including caste, regional dynamics, and ideological movements, have shaped Indian politics. National parties have historically adopted a broad-based appeal, while regional parties have often mobilized specific identity groups. The evolution of this dynamic can be understood through the power shifts seen in various states.

Take Uttar Pradesh, often regarded as the epicenter of Indian politics. The rise of the Samajwadi Party (SP) and Bahujan Samaj Party (BSP) was not just about ideology; it was about the mobilization of caste and community-based groups. The SP capitalized on Yadav-Muslim solidarity, while the BSP unified Dalits under Kanshi Ram and Mayawati's leadership. Then came the Bharatiya Janata Party (BJP), which realigned the political order by consolidating multiple social groups under the broader Hindutva narrative. These shifts demonstrate that while caste is a significant factor, broader ideological and governance-related narratives also shape electoral outcomes.

Now, shift your gaze to Tamil Nadu, a state that prides itself on progressive politics. The Dravidian movement, led by leaders like Periyar and later CN Annadurai, was a direct challenge to upper-caste dominance. Over time, however, political mobilization in the state has continued to be influenced by various social identities. Thevars, Vanniyars, Gounders—each group has found its space in the power structure. The irony? A movement that sought to dismantle caste barriers ended up institutionalizing new forms of identity-based politics.

So, does a voter today choose a candidate based on caste? The answer is layered. Some vote explicitly on identity lines, seeing their leader as their only hope for representation. Others, even if they claim to be above identity politics, subconsciously lean toward candidates who reflect their community's aspirations. Yet, there is also a growing section of the electorate that prioritizes governance, development, and leadership effectiveness over identity-based considerations. The Indian voter is evolving, balancing multiple factors before casting their ballot.

Role of Identity and Policy in Election Manifestos

If you really want to understand how political parties appeal to different voter groups, look no further than election manifestos. They are not just policy documents; they are strategic roadmaps designed to secure electoral support.

Consider this: before elections, political parties announce a mix of economic reforms, job creation plans, infrastructure promises, and targeted welfare measures. While some initiatives cater to specific communities, others aim at broad-based development. The BSP and DMK, for instance, have built their ideological foundation on social justice, while the BJP has strategically expanded its appeal to multiple communities. Similarly, Congress, over the years, has balanced welfare policies with promises of inclusive governance.

Identity-based policies, which the Constitution sought to balance through social justice mechanisms, have evolved within democratic politics. While electoral democracy has provided marginalized communities a platform for representation, it has also led to competitive identity politics.

Impact of Social Media and Awareness on Elections

There was a time when political mobilization occurred primarily through rallies, print media, and grassroots networks. Today, the battlefield has shifted. Walk into the digital sphere, and you'll see narratives being reinforced, countered, and debated in real-time. Social media has become a powerful tool, influencing voter sentiment across diverse groups.

Platforms like Twitter, Facebook, and WhatsApp have become breeding grounds for political discourse. Carefully crafted messages, videos, and infographics are circulated to shape public opinion. Political strategists understand the power of digital engagement, and no election today is complete without targeted online outreach.

Yet, with this rise in digital awareness, a countercurrent is emerging. A new generation of voters is challenging conventional vote-bank politics. They are no longer swayed solely by traditional identity markers but are demanding governance rooted in merit, transparency, and accountability.

These shifts in voter consciousness signal a growing demand for politics that prioritize development over narrow electoral strategies.

The Evolving Nature of Indian Democracy

The evolving nature of Indian democracy indeed presents a fascinating paradox, where the interplay of identity politics and governance-focused aspirations creates a dynamic political landscape. Identity-based factors like caste, religion, and community have long shaped electoral outcomes, influencing voters' preferences and political alignments. Yet, in recent times, there has been a noticeable shift towards governance, with increasing demands for economic growth, infrastructure development, and policy-driven leadership.

This dual focus—representing both social identities and aspirations for good governance—has forced political parties to recalibrate their strategies. They now navigate a delicate balance, appealing to voters based on shared identities while also addressing concerns about effective leadership and developmental promises.

Indian democracy, with its vast diversity and unique social fabric, certainly stands out not just in terms of its scale, but also its complexity. The evolving political consciousness among voters, where expectations are not limited to traditional identities but expand to include aspirations for better governance, reflects a sophisticated and mature democracy.

This complexity also makes India's democracy a dynamic process, where each election is a reflection of the changing aspirations of its people, and each voter is looking for both representation and tangible progress. In many ways, this duality enriches the democratic experience, making it both challenging and invigorating.

So, the next time you hear someone say that Indian democracy is the world's largest, remember: it is also one of the most complex. Because here, elections are not just about governance—they are about aspirations, representation, and the evolving nature of political consciousness.

Reservation and Electoral Representation

Let's talk about something that touches the heart of India's democracy: *reservation* and its role in our electoral system. It's a subject that often sparks debates, emotions, and opinions—so, let's dive into the complexities together.

You might already know that India's electoral system has special provisions for Scheduled Castes (SC), Scheduled Tribes (ST), and Other Backward Classes (OBC), ensuring they are represented in legislative bodies. This was a crucial step towards making India's democracy more inclusive, especially considering our long history of discrimination. But the story doesn't end there, does it?

1. SC, ST, and OBC Representation in Elections

Think back to the days of pre-Independence India, where social hierarchies were deeply embedded in every aspect of life. Dalits, Adivasis, and those belonging to backward castes were not just excluded from political processes; they were also oppressed and marginalized in society. The Constitution of India, however, decided to change the course of history by granting them reservations to ensure they had a voice in governance.

For many from these communities, this wasn't just about representation—it was a lifeline. A chance to break free from centuries of silence and start contributing to a democratic society. Over the decades, this system has played a key role in bringing people from these marginalized communities into the corridors of power. They have been able to raise issues that affect them, from education to healthcare to rural development, putting the spotlight on their unique struggles.

But, even with all this, there's always the question: *Has this been enough?* Are we truly seeing empowerment, or is it just a token presence in the political space?

2. Debate on Extending Reservations in Elections

Now, let's talk about the ongoing debate surrounding the extension of reservations. It's a tough one. You'll often hear opinions flying left and right—*"Reservations should be extended to more groups!"* or *"Enough with reservations, it's time to focus on merit!"*

I recently had a conversation with a friend who was deeply frustrated by the idea of reservations. "Why should someone be given a position just because of their caste?" she asked. While I understand her frustration, it made me think about the deep-rooted inequalities that still persist in our society.

The fact is, caste-based discrimination isn't something that vanishes overnight. Even today, millions of people from SC, ST, and OBC communities face barriers that prevent them from accessing education, healthcare, and opportunities that others take for granted. The reservation system, for all its flaws, remains a tool for lifting these groups from the margins and allowing them to compete on a more equal footing.

But does this mean we should expand reservations to every possible group? Extending reservations could potentially further divide the society based on caste, rather than unite it. While we need policies to empower the marginalized, there is a growing concern that too much focus on caste-based reservations might reduce the incentive for creating a more merit-based system. How do we find that balance?

3. Political Empowerment vs. Tokenism

Here's where the real conversation begins—*empowerment or tokenism?*

When you look at SC, ST, and OBC representation in elections, the question is: Are these leaders truly empowered, or are they merely symbols of political correctness? Sure, we have more representatives from these communities in Parliament and state assemblies than ever before. But what does this representation really mean?

There's an anecdote I remember from a few years ago, during a state election in Tamil Nadu. A prominent leader from a backward community was elected with great fanfare, hailed as a victory for social justice. But when the time came for him to voice issues affecting his community—like poverty, access to education, or social security—he was quickly overshadowed by the larger political machinery. His presence felt more like a checkbox ticked by the party, rather than someone truly speaking for his people.

This is where tokenism comes in. It's when a community's voice is used for political gain but not given the real power to create change. The problem isn't the reservation itself, but whether these leaders actually have the freedom and capacity to shape policies that make a difference. It's one thing to be in the room; it's another to hold the pen that writes the policies.

So, what is the solution? The key lies in true political empowerment. It's not just about holding office—it's about having the tools, the resources, and the influence to make real decisions that benefit one's community. Representation shouldn't be a symbolic gesture. It should lead to substantial change in the lives of those who need it most.

As we think about this complex issue, it's clear that the debate on reservations in elections isn't going anywhere anytime soon. It's a reflection of the larger struggle for social justice, identity, and equality in India. The question, then, isn't just whether we should have reservations, but how we can make them work better, so that everyone gets a fair chance, without perpetuating divisions or reducing people to mere representatives of their caste.

Because, ultimately, elections in India aren't just about governance—they are about aspirations, representation, and the ever-evolving consciousness of a democracy that is, at once, the world's largest and one of its most intricate.

Caste and Coalition Politics: The Unspoken Story of India's Democracy

Imagine you're standing in a busy election rally in Bihar or Uttar Pradesh, surrounded by the vibrancy of hundreds of supporters waving flags and chanting slogans. It's easy to get lost in the noise—the colorful faces, the dramatic speeches, the promises of a better future. But behind all the pageantry lies a much deeper, often unspoken truth: the electoral game in India is never just about policies or governance. It's about caste.

Now, I know what you might be thinking—*Caste again?* Isn't it a thing of the past? Shouldn't we be focusing on development, economic growth, and progress? Well, here's the thing: caste politics are not just surviving; they're thriving, shaping how alliances are formed and governments are built.

Let me take you deeper into the world of caste and coalition politics, where every vote has a backstory, and every alliance tells a tale of ambition, survival, and sometimes, sheer pragmatism.

The Political Dance of Caste Alliances: A Story of Survival

I want to take you back to 2017. The Samajwadi Party (SP) and Congress decided to come together in Uttar Pradesh for the state assembly elections. On paper, this made sense. The SP, led by the Yadav community, had long been the dominant party in the state, while Congress was hoping to tap into the Muslim vote, another strong community in the region. But as the campaign unfolded, something interesting happened. It wasn't just about the promises of good governance that kept the crowds coming; it was the recognition of the caste affiliations they represented.

Here's where the story gets interesting. While the SP was primarily focused on consolidating the Yadav vote bank, Congress aimed to secure the Muslim vote, traditionally loyal to the party. But there was another layer to this—an undercurrent of smaller caste groups who had started to feel neglected. The real battle wasn't just about two major political parties—*it was about the caste groups whose interests were being represented* in this delicate political tango.

Now, imagine this scene: a crowd of people, each person with a different expectation—some wanted better schools, others better roads, and many wanted their caste identity to be recognized in the state's politics. The power of these caste groups couldn't be ignored. It was like the very foundation of the alliance was built on understanding which caste communities were being left out, which ones needed the most attention, and which ones held the balance of power. The rally wasn't just a call for political change—it was a desperate plea for recognition and a chance at power.

The Anatomy of a Coalition: When Caste Becomes Currency

But let's step back and think about the bigger picture for a moment. You might be asking, *Why does this matter?* Why is caste so central to coalitions? The answer lies in the *math* of Indian politics.

Look at the 2019 Lok Sabha elections in Bihar, where the Rashtriya Janata Dal (RJD) joined forces with the Congress, Janata Dal (United)

(JD(U)), and several smaller caste-based parties in what was called the "Mahagathbandhan" (Grand Alliance). This wasn't just a coalition built on political ideology or governance promises—it was a calculated maneuver to create an unbreakable caste-based vote bank.

The caste-based strategy was so deeply ingrained that the leaders didn't even need to say much in their speeches. Their presence alone signified an unspoken promise to cater to specific caste groups—the Yadavs, Muslims, and other OBCs—who would deliver the crucial votes needed for the coalition to survive. But the fragility of these coalitions became apparent as the election approached. The caste-based groups that the alliance relied on weren't just a homogenous mass of voters—they were diverse, with different aspirations, and often conflicting interests.

What happens when these votes aren't delivered as expected? The cracks begin to show. For example, in the 2019 Bihar elections, even within the Mahagathbandhan, some caste groups felt sidelined, and the delicate balance started to collapse. It's like a house of cards, each card representing a caste interest. One wrong move, and the entire structure can fall apart.

When Caste Politics Defines Governance

Now, let's think about how these caste-based coalitions influence governance. When governments are formed in states like Bihar, Uttar. Pradesh, and Tamil Nadu, the cabinet decisions, the policy directions, and even the distribution of resources often come down to caste-based considerations. You might hear terms like "seats" and "power-sharing," but behind those discussions lie the needs of specific caste communities.

Take Bihar again. The influence of caste in shaping the local governance is undeniable. Here, the RJD's leader, Lalu Prasad Yadav, has built his political empire around the consolidation of the Yadav vote bank. But here's the twist: It's not just about *one* caste group—it's about ensuring that other castes, especially the backward classes and Muslims, are part of the political narrative. The moment these groups feel left out or overlooked, the alliance crumbles. The government, in turn, starts to face the risk of losing its political legitimacy.

But the problem is deeper. In these coalitions, governance often takes a backseat to the politics of representation. Ministers from these caste-based groups often push for policies that benefit their specific communities rather than the state as a whole. While this isn't necessarily a bad thing, it creates a sense of political fragmentation. The result? You end up with governments that are more about keeping the coalition intact than about actually governing for the greater good.

In India's ever-evolving political landscape, the convergence of caste, media, and digital campaigns has redefined how voters engage with democracy. While the post-independence model focused primarily on identity-based politics, a significant shift is occurring, where governance and policies now play a pivotal role in shaping public discourse. The rise of digital media, social influencers, and campaigns like #MainBhiChowkidar and #ModiHaiTohMumkinHai, have not only mobilized voters but have also sparked new forms of political consciousness, particularly among young voters. This shift underscores a transition where political allegiance is increasingly tied to tangible results rather than just identity-based politics.

However, this transformation isn't devoid of challenges. Despite digital progress, India's political fabric remains deeply embedded in social hierarchies, making it crucial to ensure that technology doesn't exacerbate existing inequalities. Recent state elections have showcased this duality, where social media campaigns, such as those in Tamil Nadu and Uttar Pradesh, have successfully elevated governance-based narratives alongside identity politics. Yet, issues like caste-based reservation and religious divides continue to influence voting patterns significantly.

Reflecting on these dynamics, my own understanding of democracy's future has been deeply shaped by my experiences with my community and the ideals I engage with at All for All. As we move towards a more tech-savvy electorate, it becomes essential for future political leadership to strike a balance between leveraging digital tools for progress and preserving the integrity of our inclusive democratic values. This balance will ultimately determine how India navigates its complex political landscape in the decades to come.

The Power of the Smaller Caste-Based Parties

You may wonder why some smaller caste-based parties seem to wield disproportionate power. Let me share a powerful example: the role of smaller parties like the Lok Janshakti Party (LJP) in Bihar. In 2014, the LJP, led by Ram Vilas Paswan, entered into an alliance with the BJP, representing the Dalit vote bank. This seemingly small party ended up playing a pivotal role in the state's politics, especially during the 2014 and 2019 elections. By representing a specific caste group, the LJP became a key ally in the coalition government, influencing decisions on everything from policy to resource allocation.

These smaller parties are often the glue that holds coalitions together. Their support can make or break a government. So, when you hear about political negotiations happening behind the scenes—it's not just about ideology, but about making sure every caste group gets their due.

The Future of Caste in Coalition Politics

As we look toward the future, it's clear that caste will continue to play a crucial role in coalition politics. But there's a growing undercurrent of change. As younger generations become more educated, more exposed to global ideas, and more focused on development, the traditional caste-based alliances might evolve. There's a rising demand for better governance, and many voters are beginning to prioritize economic growth, education, and healthcare over purely caste-based considerations.

However, we're not there yet. The reality is that for now, caste-based coalitions remain the cornerstone of Indian politics. And for anyone involved in the political process, understanding this reality is crucial. It's about acknowledging that caste is not just a relic of the past, but a living, breathing force that shapes how political alliances are forged and governments are formed.

So, as you head into the voting booth in the next election, remember this: the political landscape is shaped by much more than just the candidates or their promises. It's shaped by the intricate web of caste, identity, and coalitions. And understanding this will not only help you vote with more awareness but also help you understand the complex beauty of Indian democracy.

Legal and Constitutional Aspects: Caste and the Law in Indian Elections

India's democracy is like a vast, intricate tapestry, with countless threads woven from its history, culture, and politics. And somewhere in the middle of it all, caste plays a role that we cannot ignore. But there's something else woven in—the **law**—a structure designed to ensure fairness, equality, and accountability in the midst of this intricate web. The problem, however, is that while **caste** and **identity** play a prominent role in shaping our electoral landscape, the law is often in a constant struggle to regulate it in a way that fosters true democratic participation. So, let's take a deeper dive into the ways the **Election Commission of India** and the **Supreme Court** have attempted to tackle this complex issue of caste and elections. And trust me, it's not as straightforward as it seems.

Election Commission Regulations: Striking a Fine Balance

I want you to imagine this scenario: It's election season. Political rallies are happening everywhere, the streets are flooded with posters, and the air is filled with promises. And in the midst of it all, a politician gets on stage and says something like, *"We need to vote for people of our own community to ensure our share in development."* At first glance, this might sound like a rallying cry for empowerment. But when you step back and look at it from a legal perspective, you realize that this kind of speech crosses a line. It becomes a **corrupt practice**, an attempt to sway votes based solely on caste, and that's where the **Election Commission of India (ECI)** comes in.

The **Representation of the People Act, 1951**, lays down the rules of the game. Section 123(3) explicitly bans any form of caste-based campaigning, considering it a **corrupt practice**. This means that if a candidate or party appeals to voters based on their caste, religion, or community, they could face disqualification. Seems clear-cut, right? Well, it's not.

In theory, the Election Commission is the watchdog, stepping in when political parties or candidates overstep these boundaries. They issue warnings, send notices, or even cancel nominations if necessary. However, enforcement isn't always black and white. Political parties and candidates are often very **strategic** in how they approach caste. They may not explicitly ask for votes based on caste, but they will create **alliances** with certain groups, give tickets to candidates from specific communities, or make subtle references that resonate deeply with caste-based sentiments.

Take, for example, the case of the **Bihar elections** a few years ago. Political parties *didn't explicitly* make caste-based appeals in their speeches, but when it came to **ticket distribution**, the parties made sure that the candidates who had the strongest support from particular caste groups were the ones chosen. Caste wasn't mentioned directly, but its presence was everywhere—in the candidate selection, the campaign strategies, and even in the alliances formed. This is a common pattern in many elections, whether we're talking about the North, South, East, or West of India. Caste-based politics might not always be overt, but it's deeply entrenched, making the role of the ECI even more challenging.

Supreme Court Rulings: The Fine Line Between Reality and Idealism

Now, let's move to the **Supreme Court of India**. The Court has been at the heart of shaping legal interpretations of caste in elections. It has ruled on several cases that attempt to balance the practical reality of caste-based voting with the constitutional vision of an egalitarian society. One of the landmark rulings came in the **Abhiram Singh v. C.D. Commachen (2017)** case, where a seven-judge bench made a powerful statement: appealing to voters on the basis of caste or religion is **illegal**, even if it's done in a roundabout way.

The judgment clarified that **"seeking votes based on caste"** falls under the category of **corrupt practices**, and anyone found guilty of such tactics could face disqualification. On the surface, this sounds like a victory for a secular, caste-neutral India. But here's the catch—the Court may have laid down the law, but how do you apply it when caste and community are so **deeply ingrained** in the political fabric of our country?

Think about it—**caste is not just a social category in India**; it's a **lived experience**. It defines people's lives in ways that affect their education, employment, and even marriage choices. It shapes their sense of belonging. So, can you really disconnect this deeply rooted social identity from the political sphere? The Court tried to do that, but the ground reality is complicated.

Let me tell you a little story to illustrate this.

Back in the 1990s, when the **Mandal Commission Report** was implemented, the country saw massive protests, and for the first time, caste-based reservations were **officially recognized** in public sector jobs and educational institutions. Now, what was the political fallout of this? Political parties began to see **OBCs (Other Backward Classes)** as an important vote bank, and caste, which had always been at the heart of rural politics, exploded onto the national scene. Parties started **basing their campaigns** on caste, not only in terms of reservations but also in terms of **representation**. They began saying things like, *"A vote for us is a vote for your caste."*

While the Supreme Court didn't explicitly endorse caste-based mobilization, it **reinforced the political logic** of caste when it upheld **reservations for OBCs**. This meant that while the law was trying to contain caste-based appeals, the very **structure** of the political system was giving caste even more power.

The Grey Area: When Law Meets Reality

Here's the thing—**caste doesn't play by the law**. No matter how much we try to regulate it, caste keeps influencing our elections. And the reason for that lies in the social dynamics of India. **Caste-based vote banks** are real. The notion of caste as a **source of identity and power** is so ingrained that it becomes difficult to erase from the political conversation. **Voters** align themselves with parties that represent their **caste interests**, even if they're not explicitly told to do so.

Let me take you to the streets of a small town in Uttar Pradesh. It's election time, and candidates from different political parties are out on their rallies. If you listen closely to their speeches, you'll hear them talking about **development** and **jobs**. But then, in the middle of their speech, they'll mention something like, *"This government has always looked after the interests of people like you."* In this statement, "people like you" is a reference to a specific **caste group**, even though it's not stated explicitly. Voters understand it. It works. Why? Because the bond between caste and **representation** is deep.

What Does the Future Hold?

As we look to the future, the question remains: Can we change the political landscape and move away from **caste-based politics**? **Is the law powerful enough to regulate caste?** Or do we need a **revolution in consciousness**, where we begin to **look at elections beyond caste**—to focus on governance, policies, and representation that is based on the **common good**, rather than identity?

The law can only do so much. The **real challenge** lies in changing the mindset of both **politicians** and **voters**. **Caste** will always play a role in politics, but can we ensure that it plays a smaller role? Can we demand a future where politicians **compete on the basis of policies** and not caste? Maybe it's time to shift the focus. **We, as voters**, need to look at **issues beyond caste** and demand better governance. It's time for us to move from **vote banks** to **policy banks**.

Is that a dream or a possibility? That's for all of us to decide, but I believe the power lies in our hands—**in the way we cast our votes**, in the way we choose to look at elections.

So, the question is: **Will we make caste a thing of the past, or will it continue to shape our political future?**

The Role of the Law in Promoting Upliftment: A Step Toward Change

Let's not lose sight of the most powerful force in this discussion: the Indian Constitution. The framers of the Constitution envisioned a country where caste-based discrimination was eradicated, and every individual had the right to equal opportunities. The reservation system, while debated, has served as an important tool for uplifting marginalized communities, ensuring they have a place in education, employment, and politics. These legal protections aren't about perpetuating caste identity; they're about creating access to resources and opportunities that have historically been denied.

Take, for example, the rise of Dalit leaders in recent decades. The Election Commission's role is to ensure that campaigns focus on issues that benefit all sections of society, but at the same time, there's an inherent understanding that elevating marginalized communities is still part of the work that needs to be done. It's why we've seen parties like BSP (Bahujan Samaj Party), led by leaders like Mayawati, make significant strides in representing Dalit interests. These leaders aren't just token figures—they're symbols of empowerment in action, showing that caste-based identities can be reframed as political power for social and economic upliftment.

One of the most encouraging examples of this shift can be seen in the education sector. The implementation of reservation policies for Scheduled Castes (SC), Scheduled Tribes (ST), and Other Backward Classes (OBCs) has helped create opportunities for young people from marginalized communities to access higher education. Today, we see more and more individuals from these communities becoming doctors, engineers, teachers, and bureaucrats—positions that were once inaccessible. The changing educational landscape is proof that caste-based reservations, in their current form, are tools of social upliftment rather than mere political leverage.

Political Empowerment and Social Upliftment: Bridging the Gap

But there's another side to this coin. The question we need to ask is: *Is caste still necessary for empowerment, or can we look at class-based politics—policies that focus on poverty, access to resources, and general well-being—to bring about the kind of changes that lift people out of their circumstances?*

Here's where the future of Indian democracy lies: It's in bridging the gap between caste-based mobilization and universal social progress. I want to bring you back to that small town in Uttar Pradesh, where the voices of political leaders are intertwined with caste, but there's something else happening, something you don't hear in the speeches. The youth of these communities are no longer just looking for representation; they are looking for opportunities. They are asking for policies that will improve healthcare, education, and job prospects, regardless of caste.

Take, for example, the success stories of Dalit entrepreneurs in urban areas—young minds who are creating businesses, forging alliances, and pursuing careers that don't rely on the legacy of caste to succeed. One such story is of Udhay Kumar, a Dalit from Tamil Nadu, who, despite coming from a small village, went on to start a successful tech company. His story is a powerful reminder that social mobility is real, and caste need not limit one's potential if the right opportunities are given.

And we must acknowledge the positive changes happening with the advent of urbanization and education. The younger generation is more connected than ever before, and the impact of social media and education on caste perceptions is profound. The more educated and

urbanized people become, the more open-minded they tend to be about issues like caste. This is why many young voters today are more likely to vote for policies and ideas that transcend caste divisions

Legal and Constitutional Aspects: Caste, Law, and the Future of Upliftment

Imagine you're walking down a bustling street in a small town, the air is thick with the **vibrancy of elections**. The billboards, the loudspeakers, the political rallies—everything feels electric. But then, in the midst of all the noise, someone hands you a pamphlet. It reads: *"Vote for a government that will lift communities out of poverty, where caste doesn't define your future."* For a moment, it catches your attention. It's a reminder that **India's politics is evolving**, shifting from **representation by caste** to a more progressive narrative: **representation by needs, aspirations, and policies**.

That pamphlet represents the future—a future where caste, while still a reality in many ways, **doesn't have to be the sole driver of political identity**. The law, the courts, and even political parties are slowly, but steadily, trying to reframe the conversation. And here's the thing: this **shift** isn't just about politics—it's about **empowerment, progress, and change**. **Caste may still be there, but it no longer has to define who gets access to opportunities.**

The Road Ahead for Caste in Indian Electoral Politics

As we wrap up this conversation on the intersection of caste and electoral politics in India, it's vital to zoom out and reflect on the bigger picture. The political journey we're navigating today is nothing short of fascinating—a **complex web** where **caste** plays a pivotal role, but is no longer the sole driver of political change. What we're witnessing isn't just a continuation of old trends, but a shift in the **core dynamics** of Indian politics.

Caste has always been a **significant factor** in shaping political strategies. Yet, we are now at a crossroads where it seems that **identity politics** is giving way to something deeper—**a hunger for progress**. There's an increasing recognition that, while caste may still influence voter behavior in certain pockets, the real drivers of politics today are **governance**, **policy**, and **the quest for a better life**. Voters, especially the youth, are demanding **tangible change**—whether it's better healthcare, better education, or economic opportunities—not just the promises that have been tied to caste-based vote banks for decades.

But here's the interesting part—this doesn't mean that caste's role is disappearing. It's evolving. Rather than just being a tool for political mobilization, caste is now becoming part of a **larger narrative** of empowerment and representation. The system of **reservation**, which once emerged as a mechanism for social justice, is now being discussed in the context of **empowering marginalized communities through opportunity**, not just votes. In a country as diverse as India, **representation** is still important—but it's **representation for empowerment**, not just identity politics for its own sake.

The future of caste in electoral politics isn't about completely removing its influence. It's about **redefining it**—from something that divides to something that can uplift. We need to ask ourselves: **how do we move from tokenism to true empowerment?** How do we build a society where the benefits of **economic growth**, **social development**, and **education** can transcend caste-based barriers, and where leadership is based on **merit**, **vision**, and **policies** that can address **every citizen's needs**, regardless of background?

Equality should be the guiding principle in shaping our democracy. We are moving towards a time when **no one's potential should be limited by their caste**, and no one should be left behind simply because of where they were born or what their ancestors faced. **Everyone**, regardless of their identity, should have the same chance to thrive, to succeed, and to contribute to the growth of this nation.

This is where true progress lies—not in perpetuating the divisions of the past but in creating a system that prioritizes **equal access to education**, **equal representation**, and **equal economic opportunities**. The question isn't just about removing caste from electoral politics—it's about **creating a society where caste doesn't matter anymore**. We must work towards **policies that are centered on merit, capability, and need**, not identity.

Possible Reforms for a More Inclusive Political System

For India to truly evolve and for the caste-based politics to give way to something better, we need reforms that aren't just **paper-based** but **life-changing**. These reforms have to be embedded in the fabric of our society—politically, socially, and economically. Here's how we can start building that future:

1. Shifting the Focus to Issue-Based Politics:

Picture this: an election season where political parties are **competing not for caste votes** but for the **best healthcare policies**, **best educational reforms**, and **most impactful economic opportunities**. This isn't a utopian dream; it's a possible reality. Political campaigns need to shift from identity-based appeals to issue-based campaigns that promise tangible changes. Imagine a voter no longer casting their ballot based on who they are told they should vote for, but based on what matters most to them—whether it's a new hospital in their locality, better roads, or more jobs. **When politics is about the future we can build together, caste stops becoming the focal point.**

2. Enhancing Merit-Based Representation with Social Justice:

It's time we build a system where **merit** and **social justice** are not seen as opposites, but as **complementary goals**. While reservations have their place in correcting historical wrongs, let's start envisioning a future where **merit is not defined by caste**, but by the **skills, passion, and hard work** someone brings to the table. For instance, imagine students from marginalized communities entering prestigious universities, **not because of their caste**, but because they have the **resources and opportunities** to succeed. As we move forward, we can work towards a system that encourages and nurtures talent from all walks of life, while still ensuring that **no community is left behind**.

3. Economic Upliftment: The True Game-Changer

You know what would truly bring equality? **Economic empowerment.** Think about this: if **economic mobility** were at the heart of India's policies, caste would start becoming irrelevant. **Economic justice** means access to good education, better jobs, healthcare, and affordable housing. This is the kind of change that directly impacts people's lives. Picture a young person from a rural village, not bound by the limitations of their caste but empowered by **job opportunities**, **skill-building programs**, and **access to resources** that allow them to **dream big**. Over time, when individuals have the **economic freedom** to shape their destinies, **caste-based identification will weaken**.

4. The Power of Education and Awareness:

What if, in the future, our children were raised not with the mindset of 'What caste are you?' but with 'What are your dreams?' **Education** will be the key that unlocks this future. Imagine a society where schools and universities emphasize social cohesion, where children learn not just about their own culture, but about **respect for all cultures**, and **recognizing each individual for their unique capabilities**. Public awareness campaigns must emphasize this: **caste doesn't determine your worth**, but your contributions to society do. Over time, the narratives of **division** will be replaced with **stories of unity and progress**.

5. **Legal and Constitutional Reforms: Enforcing Equality in the True Sense:**

India's Constitution already guarantees equality, but **laws** must evolve to reflect the realities of modern-day politics. We don't need more laws that just sit there and get ignored—we need laws that create **real consequences** for caste-based discrimination in elections. What if we had stronger judicial actions and reforms that made it **illegal to play the caste card** in elections? That would immediately shift the political narrative. The role of the **Election Commission** must go beyond just overseeing elections—it needs to be a **guardian of inclusivity**, ensuring that political rhetoric is **rooted in policy** and not in old divides. A constitutional overhaul could allow for a future where **elections are driven by the future**, not the past.

The Big Picture: Beyond Caste, Towards Equality

When we think about these reforms, it's important to zoom out and think of the **big picture**. It's not just about creating laws or changing political strategies; it's about a **shift in how we view each other**. Imagine a future where caste is not just irrelevant in politics but also in daily life. What if someone from a historically marginalized community had the same **opportunities, access, and treatment** as someone from a so-called "privileged" background? Imagine the kind of India we could build if we prioritize **equality**, not just in politics but in **every corner of our lives**.

We have the tools to get there—we just need the vision to understand that **true equality** is the **only true change**. **Reforms** aren't just about policy—they're about **empowering people** and **creating a world where no one is left behind**, regardless of their caste, creed, or background. This is the reform we need, and it's the one that will set India on the path to a more just and equal democracy.

At the heart of this transformation lies the understanding that **no one should be treated as a token or a number**. Every citizen deserves the chance to rise on their own merits, to have their voice heard, and to be included in the democratic process. This is the India we should strive for—a country where **equality** is not just an aspiration, but a **fundamental right**.

We've made progress, but the work isn't done yet. We must move beyond **identity-based mobilization** and focus on what truly matters: **creating a level playing field** for all. It's about designing policies that aren't just about **representation** but are about **empowerment**—policies that provide everyone with the resources and opportunities to reach their full potential. Whether it's through better **education**, **job creation**, or **economic mobility**, **equality** must be at the core of every decision we make.

The future of Indian democracy should not be about reinforcing old divisions; it should be about fostering a society where **everyone**—regardless of their caste, religion, or background—can walk together on equal footing. We can't afford to look at our differences as barriers; we must look at them as part of a **diverse, vibrant whole** that can only flourish when equality becomes the central pillar.

In the end, the future of caste in Indian politics isn't about abolishing it from our discussions—it's about **transforming the political and social system to a place where caste is no longer a factor** in determining someone's worth or their future. Let's focus on **equality**—because, ultimately, **everyone deserves to be equal**.

HOW FAR HAS INDIA COME?

> *"A democratic form of government presupposes a democratic form of society."*
>
> **-Dr. BR. Ambedkar**

Let me take you on a journey—not through the history books you've read, but through the stories you haven't heard. Stories not of statistics, but of real people—the ones whose names we don't always remember, but whose lives carry the weight of this nation's unfinished promise.

Take, for instance, the story of Raghavan, an old man I met while volunteering in a small village. His skin was weathered, like an ancient tree, and his eyes still sharp, despite the years. He was born into a community burdened by centuries of discrimination. His father, too, had been a laborer, toiling away in the fields of a landlord whose name no one dared speak aloud. But Raghavan? He broke that cycle. He got an education, fought for his right to own land, and led a small group of activists who managed to push the boundaries of what seemed impossible. And yet, when I asked him what had changed, he paused.

"It's different now," he said, looking into the distance, "but not by much. The walls have changed, but they're still here. You can see them, but you've learned to look away."

I sat there, feeling the weight of his words. In that moment, it wasn't just his story—I felt it in my own life too. How often had I seen progress framed in grand terms, only to realize that what had truly shifted were the boundaries, not the foundation? The walls may not be as obvious, but they're still there, in the way people talk, the way they look at you, the way they place you into boxes before you've even had a chance to speak. I thought about how, in our rush to celebrate victories, we sometimes forget that real change is about breaking down the walls, not just decorating them. And perhaps that's where India still struggles—how can we say we've progressed if we've only learned to mask the walls, rather than dismantle them altogether?

The Village That Time Left Behind

Gaurav Kumar, a Dalit student from a village near Kanpur, Uttar Pradesh, was a brilliant student who topped his school exams in 2014. Instead of being celebrated, his success was met with hostility and discrimination. His academic achievements were seen as a threat to the caste hierarchy in his village. Teachers and peers turned against him, and his family faced threats and social isolation. Gaurav's father, a sanitation worker, was denied basic rights, such as participating in village meetings, while the community imposed a complete social boycott on his family.

The discrimination intensified when Gaurav applied for a scholarship reserved for Dalit students. Despite his top marks, upper-caste families protested, claiming he didn't deserve the scholarship. Gaurav's case highlighted the harsh reality faced by Dalit students—no matter how hard they work, their achievements are often overshadowed by their caste. This is not just Gaurav's story but the reality for many Dalit students in India, who face constant challenges in an education system that still measures their worth by their caste, not their ability.

In the village of Perundheru, Tamil Nadu, caste divides not just communities but futures. On February 22nd, 14-year-old Chinnadurai and his younger sister became victims of violent caste-based hatred. Chinnadurai, a Dalit student, was brutally attacked by his classmates simply for standing tall and excelling, while his sister was also beaten for being by his side. The attack wasn't just physical—it was an assault on their dignity, a cruel reminder that in a world where caste defines everything, no matter how hard you fight, your worth is always measured by your birth.

This violence isn't isolated; it's part of a larger system that teaches children to hate and oppress from an early age. The system is broken, and while laws and policies exist, they mean little when the mindset remains unchanged. Chinnadurai and his sister's story is not an isolated tragedy—it is the reality for millions of Dalit children in India. Until we confront the deeply ingrained casteism that continues to shape our schools, communities, and laws, true equality will remain out of reach.

Take **Mari Selvaraj**, a filmmaker from Tamil Nadu who, in an interview, spoke about how his father, a sanitary worker, faced humiliation when he tried to enroll him in a "dominant caste" school. Or the tragic case of **P. Ilavarasan**, a Dalit youth from Dharmapuri, who was found dead in 2012 after marrying a Vanniyar girl, triggering caste riots in the region. His death, controversially ruled a suicide, followed intense social pressure and threats.

These are not stories from a century ago. They are the lived realities of people in an India that celebrates space missions, billion-dollar startups, and a growing economy. It is a **stark reminder that while policies change, mindsets often do not**. The real battleground isn't just in legislatures or courts—it's in villages, schools, workplaces, and homes, where caste prejudice still dictates who belongs and who does not.

The Foundation: The Indian Constitution and Its Bold Vision for Equality

When we turn the pages of the Indian Constitution, we're not just reading a legal document; we are uncovering a blueprint for a nation built on ideals of justice, equality, and fraternity. These are words we've all heard countless times—often spoken in lofty speeches, discussed in classrooms, and written in textbooks. But how often do we pause and truly question what they mean, not just in theory, but in the lived reality of millions of people across the country? The Indian Constitution, drafted by Dr. B.R. Ambedkar and his fellow visionaries, was meant to be a transformative force—one that would undo centuries of deep-rooted oppression, particularly that which had been institutionalized by the caste system.

This vision was not merely to create a framework of governance but to establish a society where no one would be judged by the circumstances of their birth. Yet, as we explore the journey of India's democracy, we must confront a critical question: how much of Ambedkar's dream has truly materialized? The Constitution's promises are undeniably revolutionary, but they are also a mirror reflecting the contradictions of our society. In this conversation, I want to delve deeper—not into what is commonly known, but into the layers beneath it. How has caste-based discrimination continued to thrive despite constitutional guarantees? What barriers are preventing Ambedkar's vision from becoming a reality? And perhaps most importantly, what can each of us do to take this vision forward?

The Bold Promise of the Indian Constitution

Let's begin by reflecting on the ideals Ambedkar embedded in the Constitution. When Ambedkar crafted this document, he had a deep understanding of the psychological and social trauma that the caste system had inflicted on generations. Imagine the weight of his task: designing a framework that could undo centuries of social injustice. The

Constitution, in its essence, is not just a set of laws but a declaration of values. Articles 14 to 18 form the cornerstone of equality, with the powerful abolition of untouchability in Article 17 standing as a symbol of the intent to heal centuries of humiliation.

But what does "equality" mean in a country like India, where caste is woven into almost every aspect of life? The Constitution's guarantees are profound on paper, but the lived experiences of Dalits, Adivasis, and backward classes tell a different story. The reality is that constitutional promises are often thwarted by deeply embedded cultural practices and prejudices that have survived generations. How can the legal right to equality be fully realized when centuries-old social structures continue to dictate people's opportunities, relationships, and even their ability to survive? This is where the conversation often gets lost. We become so focused on the legal framework that we forget to ask: how are social and cultural norms, rooted in caste, preventing the Constitution from achieving its true potential?

Practical Implementation of Ambedkar's Vision

In Ambedkar's vision, the Constitution was a tool to bring about social transformation. But let me ask you: has this transformation really taken place? Sure, there have been legal victories. Reservations in education and employment have created pathways for those who were historically excluded. The establishment of organizations like the National Commission for Scheduled Castes was a step towards ensuring their rights. Yet, if you walk through rural India or even parts of urban areas, you'll often hear whispers of discrimination—subtle, but unmistakable. It's as if the law has been a silent spectator, powerless to confront the deep-seated prejudices that lie hidden beneath the surface of our everyday lives.

Consider a small village where the people are educated and aware of their rights, but the community still refuses to sit with someone from a lower caste at a local gathering. The laws exist, but the social fabric hasn't completely shifted. In some regions, caste is still a means of asserting power, and even those who've benefitted from affirmative action often face discrimination once they step outside of their protected spaces. The promises of equality and fraternity fade when faced with the reality of local politics, where caste plays a central role in elections, in determining who gets power, and who gets to stay marginalized.

This disconnect between law and life is crucial. Legal measures like reservations or affirmative action cannot, by themselves, heal centuries of social inequality. It's not enough to legislate against untouchability; the psychological and social structures that perpetuate it need to be dismantled. And this is where Ambedkar's vision falters—because it was never meant to be a solitary legal framework. It was meant to spark a cultural revolution. But how can such a revolution take place when the same people who are supposed to enforce these laws are entrenched in caste-based thinking themselves? It's like asking someone to clean a house while they're standing knee-deep in mud.

The Struggle for Social Equality: Unveiling the Contradictions

While India has certainly made progress, the battle is far from won. In many ways, the constitutional guarantees have been successful—there are Dalit doctors, teachers, and politicians today who might never have had a chance without affirmative action. But the reality is also far more complex. We can no longer deny that caste-based discrimination is alive and well, often disguised as something else. The violence against Dalits, the continued segregation in villages, the discrimination in schools and workplaces—all point to the failure of the Constitution's promises to penetrate the daily lives of individuals.

Let me take you to a story of an encounter I had while traveling. I met a young man from a Scheduled Caste background. He had fought hard to get into a prestigious university, and after years of struggle, he had finally secured a job in a leading corporation. He was an inspiring individual—a symbol of what the Constitution promised. Yet, when I asked him about his experience in his new workplace, he shared that his colleagues, while polite, kept a distance from him. In meetings, he noticed that his ideas were often overlooked, and he sensed an invisible barrier that kept him from fully belonging. He was no longer oppressed by the system—at least not directly—but he was still marked by an invisible social force that sought to keep him in his place. This story isn't unique. It is the story of countless individuals who rise, only to find that the social norms that once kept them down have found more subtle ways of pushing them aside.

A Call to Action: Moving Beyond the Constitution

So, what does all of this mean for us today? The Indian Constitution, in its brilliance, remains the bedrock upon which we must build our future. But we cannot afford to only look to the law. If Ambedkar's dream is to become a reality, it requires more than just legal reforms. It calls for a societal transformation—a shift in the way we view and interact with one another. It requires us to interrogate our own biases, question the caste-based divisions in our lives, and challenge the everyday practices that uphold this social structure.

We have to realize that the Constitution can only do so much. The law can provide opportunities, but it is up to us, as individuals and as a society, to cultivate a culture of equality, respect, and fraternity. The change has to come from within, not just from above. Only when the Constitution's ideals permeate every aspect of life—when they are part of how we interact with our neighbors, our colleagues, and our families—will Ambedkar's vision of a truly egalitarian society come to life.

This isn't just a matter of policy; it's a matter of our humanity. The fight for equality is not something that can be relegated to law schools or political debates. It's something that must live in our hearts and minds, in our daily actions and words. So, the next time we speak of equality, let us ask ourselves—what does it really mean, and how can we ensure that the promises of the Constitution are not just words on a page, but the reality for every single person, regardless of their caste? Let's stop waiting for a revolution that may never come and start building it—quietly, steadily, in every moment. Because that's where true change begins.

Progress in Education and Employment: How Far Have We Really Come?

As I sit here reflecting on the state of India's education system and the employment landscape for marginalized communities, I am reminded of an age-old question: *Have we really come far enough?* Reservations in education and employment were supposed to be a game-changer, right? A system designed to break the centuries-old shackles of caste discrimination and give those from marginalized communities a chance to build a life free from the weight of centuries of oppression. But, as we peel back the layers of this complex issue, we realize that while some doors have been opened, others remain locked, and the journey of true equality feels far from over.

A Promised Change

Let's begin with a story that, unfortunately, is not as rare as it should be. Meet Arvind, a Dalit student from a small village in Rajasthan. Arvind was the first in his family to graduate from college, and this achievement was made possible by the reservation system—a policy that has allowed individuals from marginalized communities to access opportunities previously closed to them. Today, Arvind works in a reputable public sector company, a job his parents, who were manual laborers, could only dream of. His story is a powerful example of how reservations have opened doors and helped break the chains of economic and social inequality imposed by caste.

But the road to this success wasn't without its challenges. Despite being admitted to a prestigious university thanks to the reservation system, Arvind was keenly aware that his presence in these spaces was often questioned. The subtle whispers, the sideways glances, and the quiet judgments—these were constant companions throughout his journey. Even in progressive and supposedly merit-based environments, caste prejudice continues to linger, sometimes in invisible forms. Arvind's experience serves as a reminder that while the reservation system has provided opportunities, it's not enough to eradicate the deep-rooted caste biases that still permeate society, especially in educational institutions and workplaces.

And here's something we all need to consider: Arvind's story is not unique. There are countless others like him across India—Dalits, Adivasis, and other marginalized communities—who have fought their own battles against inequality through education. The truth is, without the provisions of affirmative action, many of these young people would have lived lives no different from that of their parents—working as manual laborers, stuck in the same cycle of poverty and exclusion. Education, and the opportunities provided by the reservation system, have given them a shot at a different life. But what remains to be seen is whether society, as a whole, is ready to fully accept these changes, or if it will continue to hold onto its prejudices, even when the system has tried to break them down.

The Reality of Equal Access: Quality Still Matters

Let's take a moment to reflect on something often overlooked in the conversation about caste-based affirmative action: the *quality* of the education that marginalized students receive. While reservations have certainly paved the way for students from Dalit and backward communities to enter prestigious institutions, the reality is far more complex. The question that lingers is not about access but about the *kind* of access. Reservations give students a seat in the classroom, but it doesn't always ensure that they are receiving the same high-quality education as their peers.

Take Arvind's story once again. Yes, he got into a top university thanks to reservations, but once inside, he realized the challenges went beyond just getting in. His education, though valuable, often felt like it was a race against time and resources. Arvind didn't have the kind of academic mentorship, peer support, or social capital that many of his classmates took for granted. These invisible barriers—social isolation, lack of guidance, and unacknowledged struggles—are not always addressed by affirmative action. What Arvind and many like him need is not just a place in the classroom but a *support system* that nurtures their potential. The fact is that while access has been granted, the *equality of experience* is far from achieved.

Now, let's talk about Priya, another student from a Dalit background. She once shared how her classmates would joke about her rural village background, about how her "unpolished" speech and "awkward" mannerisms marked her as different. Priya, despite her brilliance, often found herself at the margins of the classroom—feeling like an outsider in spaces where she was technically supposed to belong. What she said hit me hard: "I'm not treated as a student first. I'm treated as my caste first." In a room where the walls were supposed to separate knowledge from social background, Priya still felt the weight of her caste identity, constantly questioning whether she was accepted for her ability or merely tolerated because of the reservation system.

The truth is, Dalit students often face a unique set of challenges. Yes, the reservation system provides them with opportunities that their parents could only dream of, but it doesn't remove the societal biases that persist in educational institutions. Unlike students from more privileged backgrounds, Dalit students frequently lack the *unspoken advantages* that come from having family members or mentors in academia, access to extra resources, or even a network of friends who can guide them through the labyrinth of higher education. In many ways, they are left to navigate these spaces on their own, with little to no assistance from an institution that was never built for them.

And here's something we need to think about: How many of these students, despite having the potential, will eventually leave these institutions with the same disadvantages they walked in with? How many will drop out due to a lack of proper support systems? How many will be pushed out by discrimination, even if it is subtle, through peer or faculty biases? The system, while offering them a seat, hasn't yet created a truly *inclusive* environment.

Let's pause here and think about a deeper question: What if the true challenge isn't just getting Dalit students into these institutions but truly integrating them into a space that acknowledges their unique struggles? Because, ultimately, we're not just talking about numbers or statistics; we're talking about people. People who, despite receiving a seat at the table, often feel like outsiders. Their achievements aren't just academic—they're emotional, social, and psychological battles they fight every day.

The fact that Dalit students still have to fight this fight within the walls of educational institutions speaks volumes. It's not just about the reservation system. It's about a system that hasn't fully acknowledged or addressed the long-standing consequences of caste-based exclusion. The lingering bias and subtle discrimination within these academic spaces are barriers that no one talks about enough. These are the barriers that prevent the true fulfillment of a student's potential, regardless of how much talent they possess.

But, it's not all hopeless. There is change. Some universities and organizations are beginning to recognize the need for a more inclusive and supportive environment. Initiatives like mentorship programs for marginalized students, awareness campaigns, and peer support groups are steps in the right direction. However, it's a long road ahead. What we have to realize is that true equality in education is not just about getting a seat in the classroom—it's about creating an environment where every student feels like they truly belong. And that starts with rethinking how we support students from marginalized communities.

So, I'll leave you with this: Yes, the reservation system is a victory—it has opened doors. But we need to ask ourselves, as a society: Are we content with just giving marginalized students a seat at the table, or do we want to create an environment where they can thrive? Are we willing to challenge our biases and offer real support, or are we going to let them fight their battles alone?

The Unseen Barriers: Caste in Modern Education

You know, when we talk about access to education, most people think the battle is won when the doors are opened for marginalized communities. But what happens once you step inside those doors? What happens when you sit down in that classroom, surrounded by students who seem to come from a different world altogether? Let me take you a bit deeper, to the heart of what's often overlooked: **inclusion**.

We've been talking about **access**—the idea that reservations have created space for marginalized students in educational institutions that were once exclusive to the privileged. But here's the problem: access alone doesn't guarantee equality. It doesn't guarantee that once a student from a Dalit or backward community steps into that classroom, they'll be treated with the respect they deserve, or that they'll feel like they truly belong.

The Silent Exclusion: Caste in the Curriculum

The first invisible wall that these students face is in the curriculum itself. Think about it: you're a Dalit student, you've just managed to break through centuries of systemic oppression to get a seat in a prestigious institution. You're hopeful, but as you start reading your textbooks, you realize something crucial is missing—your story.

You open your history book and what do you see? Tales of kings, empires, and the great "civilizations" that shaped the nation. But where are the stories of your ancestors, the struggles they faced, the contributions they made? **Nowhere.**

Let me tell you a story that might put this into perspective. There was a student named Manju, a bright young Dalit girl studying literature at a well-known college. Her professors were proud to boast about the "classics" they taught—works by the likes of Shakespeare, Tagore, or even Wordsworth. But Manju, as an aspiring writer, found herself asking: **Where are the Dalit voices? Where are the stories of those who've been silenced for so long?**

She told me that in her entire literature course, there was not one work by a Dalit writer. Her entire education was rooted in the experiences of those who had the privilege of being heard. For Manju, this wasn't just a curriculum gap; it was a direct erasure of her identity. **How can**

you connect with something that doesn't even acknowledge your existence?

This is the reality for many marginalized students—**the lack of representation in their education system** is not just about a missed opportunity to learn from a different perspective, it's about a denial of their dignity and their humanity. **How do we expect them to thrive when their stories are relegated to the sidelines?**

Peer Discrimination: The Invisible Battle

But the real struggle doesn't always come from textbooks. It comes from the people around them—their peers. A student can be brilliant in every way, but how often does that brilliance get overshadowed by subtle biases that come not from the system, but from the very individuals they share their classrooms with?

Let me tell you about Ramesh, a brilliant student who made it into a top engineering college through reservations. He was exceptional at what he did, but every day, he faced the humiliation of being mocked by his peers for his rural accent, for his "lack of sophistication," for the way he spoke or the way he dressed.

This isn't just teasing; it's a constant reminder that, no matter how much effort you put in, how well you perform academically, **you will never truly belong**. Peer discrimination—though often subtle—is a silent killer. It undermines self-confidence, erodes self-worth, and, most importantly, makes you question if you even have a place in the world you've fought so hard to enter.

Ramesh's story isn't unique. Many students from marginalized backgrounds face this **constant battle** of proving not just their academic capability, but their very right to be in that space. It's one thing to get a seat at the table; it's another thing to have your voice heard once you're there.

The Merit Debate: Re-examining What "Merit" Truly Means

Let's move on to something that gets debated quite often: **merit**. It's a word that's used to justify a lot of things, especially when it comes to reservations. The critics argue that reservations lower the standards, that they allow students who are "less qualified" to take the spots of those who are "more deserving."

But let me ask you this: **What is merit, really?** Is merit simply about grades, exams, or performance in a standardized system? Or is it about the resources, the environment, and the opportunities one has been given to succeed? A child born into a wealthy family with access to the best schools, the best tutors, the best healthcare—they are seen as "meritorious," right? They have the "advantages" that allow them to succeed.

But what about the child who grew up in a Dalit family, with little access to any of these advantages? **Is that child any less capable?**

No. What reservations aim to do is **level the playing field**. They aren't about lowering standards; they're about **correcting the imbalance**. Because when you start a race from behind, every step is harder than the one before it. Reservations give marginalized students the chance to run alongside their peers, with the same resources, the same opportunities. But as we've discussed, **it's not enough to let them in**. We have to ensure they feel they belong, that they're supported, and that their success isn't limited by the biases of the system.

Moving Towards True Inclusion

So, here's where the conversation needs to shift. We've fought for **access**. We've fought for **representation**. But what we really need to focus on is **inclusion**. It's not enough to give someone a seat at the table; they need to feel heard. They need to be respected. They need to be included in the conversations that matter.

This isn't just about Dalit students or marginalized communities; this is a larger issue that concerns us all. The future of our society depends on how we address these inequalities. It's about **creating a system that allows everyone, regardless of their caste or background, to reach their full potential**.

Let's be honest: the road ahead is long. The barriers that still exist in our education system are deeply entrenched, and they won't disappear overnight. But what we can do is start with **acknowledging** the problem, start by opening our minds to the stories that we haven't been told, and start building a future where no one is ever made to feel like they don't belong. Let's start by asking ourselves: **How do we create a world where every student can thrive, regardless of their background?**

It's time we begin that journey—because **equality isn't just a destination; it's a path we must walk together**.

Caste and Political Representation: A Game Changer or a Double-Edged Sword?

When I look back at India's political history, I can't help but think about how deeply caste has been woven into its fabric. From the **BSP** to the **DMK**, caste-based political movements have undeniably shaped our nation's political discourse. But let's not sugarcoat the story. The reality of caste-based politics isn't just about empowerment; it's also about the subtle ways in which it can perpetuate divisions, often without us even realizing it.

As I write this, I want to draw you into a deeper conversation—one that moves beyond the usual narratives, one that questions what it means to use caste as a tool for change. I want to explore the contradictions, the underrepresented voices, and the nuanced truths about caste in political representation. Because this conversation isn't just for academics, it's for anyone who's trying to make sense of a world where caste still plays a role in how we vote, live, and understand our identity.

Critiquing the Status Quo: Is Progress Just a Mirage?

Caste-based politics was introduced as a way to uplift the marginalized, to give voice to the voiceless. On the surface, this was a well-meaning solution, and indeed, it has empowered many, bringing justice to those who were historically left behind. But let's be honest—has it always worked as intended?

I've spent a lot of time reflecting on this, especially through my work with *All for All.* We advocate for equality and social justice, but at times, I can't ignore the fact that caste-based policies can have a double-edged impact. While they have created spaces for marginalized groups to rise politically, they have also entrenched caste identities even further. This has led to a situation where caste becomes more important than other factors, like merit, collective identity, or even shared socio-economic struggles. In some ways, the very system meant to dismantle caste-based divisions might be reinforcing them.

I'm reminded of a conversation I had during one of our workshops. A young man from a marginalized caste told me how, while he was deeply grateful for the reservations that helped him gain access to education and jobs, he now felt that his identity was confined to his caste. His every success, his every struggle, was framed through that lens. At what point does a system meant to empower transform into one that limits? Is this really progress?

And so, while caste-based political representation has undeniably brought about tangible changes, it has also contributed to the **fragmentation** of society. Our politics have become less about uniting India and more about rallying a specific group around a shared identity. The "vote bank" model might have helped marginalized communities, but has it helped the nation move toward a united future? Or has it, inadvertently, made caste the defining feature of political discourse, even in our supposed progress?

Cross-National Comparisons: A Global Struggle Against Systemic Inequality

India is not alone in grappling with systems of social stratification. If you take a broader view, caste-based politics in India shares eerie similarities with **race** and **class** systems elsewhere in the world. Take the United States, for instance. The fight for civil rights by African Americans, the resistance to systemic oppression, echoes the struggles of India's Dalit communities. Both are fighting against systems that categorize people based on identities they had no say in. Both are dealing with the fallout of centuries of historical exclusion.

And it's not just the US. In South Africa, during the apartheid era, racial identity was the central organizing principle of society. Those who were classified as "non-white" were systematically excluded from economic, social, and political opportunities, much like how caste historically dictated access to power and resources in India.

What these systems have in common is this: they are **built on the premise that some people are less than others**. And even after political movements rise up against them, the very existence of these systems ensures that the fight for equality is far from over. It's like peeling an onion—you think you're done, but there's always another layer of struggle.

Hidden Stories of Empowerment: Beyond the Headlines

We often focus on the big names—the politicians, the leaders who make headlines. But the true heart of change lies with the grassroots figures, the unknown heroes who work tirelessly on the ground to create real, tangible progress.

Take **Muthulakshmi Reddy**, a lesser-known figure, for example. She fought not just for women's rights but also for the empowerment of those from marginalized castes, challenging both gender and caste hierarchies in the medical profession. While many might not know her name, her contributions were profound—she built hospitals, opened schools, and created spaces where those from marginalized backgrounds could find a place in society.

Similarly, when I think about the work I do with *All for All*, I often find inspiration in people who might not have fancy degrees or political titles but whose hearts are rooted in the idea of **selfless service**. There was a woman from a small village near Chennai who organized women in her community to fight for better wages in agricultural work. No one would recognize her if she walked down a busy street, but her work has been revolutionary in its own right.

This is the power of **hidden voices**—those who quietly, but resolutely, challenge the status quo. Their stories are often drowned out by the loud rhetoric of mainstream politics, but they carry the pulse of real change.

Personal Connection: The Intersection of Theory and Reality

I'm not just an observer here; I've lived the complexities of caste-based politics in India. I've seen it through the lens of **All for All**, a movement that thrives on the idea of social justice without any particular caste-based agenda. The work we do is about **empowering people through education, creating a space where caste doesn't dictate their worth**. Yet, time and again, I find myself confronted with the reality that caste is an undeniable force in shaping political and social opportunities.

What does it mean for a young man from a Dalit background to walk into a political gathering where caste-based organizations dominate the discourse? He may be **politically awakened**, but does he feel empowered? Or is his sense of belonging defined by his caste identity rather than his individual achievements? This is a conversation that I've had with many young people involved in *All for All*—they want to feel part of a larger national identity, not one that's fragmented by caste.

What I've learned through my experiences, especially during outreach programs, is that while caste-based politics has helped some communities, it's also created a cycle that's hard to break. **The caste identity is so deeply ingrained in how we see the world that even the fight against it becomes a reflection of the system itself**. Is there a way to shift the narrative—to move from caste-based to **class-based politics**? To empower people not just through the lens of their caste but through their common struggles, needs, and aspirations?

A Call for Unity: The Next Step in the Fight for Equality

India's political future is not just about the victories of the past. It's about where we go from here. Can we build a system where caste is no longer the primary lens through which we see people? Where a person's worth isn't tied to their caste but to their potential, their talents, and their dreams?

As we stand at this crossroads, I urge you to consider the questions I often ask myself: **Is caste-based politics the future, or is it a stepping stone?** Are we ready to create a society where no one's identity is tied to their caste but instead to their shared humanity? I truly believe that change is possible. But it requires us to **look beyond the obvious**, to **question the narratives we have been told**, and to **create spaces where everyone has the chance to thrive—no matter their caste, background, or history**

Economic Upliftment: Has Affirmative Action Transformed Economic Realities?

When we talk about affirmative action in India, it's easy to think of it as a simple solution—quotas in education, jobs, and even political representation. But, if we pause and look closer, we start to see that this approach only scratches the surface. Despite its well-meaning intentions, has affirmative action truly transformed the economic landscape for marginalized communities? Or has it merely played into the hands of the system it was meant to challenge?

Let's consider the story of Ravi, a young Dalit entrepreneur I met during one of my travels. Ravi's dream was to run a small manufacturing business, producing eco-friendly goods in his rural village. He was determined to carve out a future for himself, but the support he needed wasn't as accessible as you might expect. Government schemes intended to help entrepreneurs from marginalized backgrounds were either too bureaucratic or too narrow in scope to help Ravi's small-scale business thrive. The financial institutions that were supposed to support him with loans turned him away, citing his caste as an obstacle.

It's not that policies like reservations don't help; they do, especially in government jobs and in education. But there's a gap. We must ask: Why is there such a heavy focus on formal sectors? In rural areas, where informal economies dominate, affirmative action often feels distant. Ravi's entrepreneurial journey reflects a broader issue—the failure of policies to adapt to the realities of the informal economy. The world of entrepreneurship, especially for people from marginalized communities, remains entangled in a web of caste-based biases, and that's something that quotas and reservations don't always address.

Affirmative action also hasn't done enough to confront **informal discrimination**. In rural areas, the caste system operates in more overt, visible ways—land ownership, access to water, or permission to participate in community rituals. In urban areas, however, caste discrimination is more subtle. It's woven into social interactions, hiring practices, and even the informal networks that govern everything from housing to marriages. How many times have you heard of someone who didn't get hired for a job despite being perfectly qualified, only to realize later that caste biases were at play? We need to acknowledge that these biases often go unspoken, but they are deeply entrenched.

Policies like reservations are crucial, but they need to go hand-in-hand with broader reforms that also support marginalized communities in informal sectors. Empowerment isn't just about getting a job in a government office—it's about creating a system where **everyone** can build a life, regardless of their caste.

The Urban-Rural Divide: Caste Discrimination in Urban Areas vs. Rural India

There is a glaring contrast between how caste discrimination plays out in rural India versus urban spaces. In the rural areas, caste discrimination is raw and obvious. Untouchability practices are still alive, and caste dictates who gets to do what. In some villages, Dalits are denied access to the community well or the local temple. Their rights are dictated by centuries-old traditions, and despite legal reforms, the power structures have not changed. For someone like Jagan, a Dalit farmer I once met, the daily reality of caste meant that his family's land was systematically undervalued, his children were excluded from local schools, and even the most basic community services were denied to him.

But in cities, the situation looks different. Caste discrimination is subtler here, often hidden behind urbanization and the veneer of progress. Urban spaces may not have formal policies that bar people from living in certain neighborhoods or renting a house based on caste, but it exists. It exists in the unspoken network of "who-knows-who," in informal hiring practices, and in the way marriages are arranged. It's not in the public eye, and it's not formalized—but it's real. Caste is often used as a tool to **privilege** certain people while **excluding** others.

This dynamic plays out, for example, in housing societies in metropolitan cities. A Dalit individual might find themselves rejected from an apartment simply because of their caste, though no one will say it outright. The rejection is wrapped up in other, more socially acceptable reasons: "Oh, it's just that they have a different lifestyle," or "The neighborhood isn't quite right for them." This has led to a phenomenon where caste discrimination is as much about **who gets access to space** as it is about **who doesn't**. It's an exclusion that, though not as physically violent as rural discrimination, still cuts deep.

An interesting case came up when a Dalit woman I know, a university professor, moved to a new city for a job. Her colleagues were friendly enough in public but when it came to the topic of marriage, things shifted. Suddenly, caste was no longer something people talked about, but it was still felt. The higher-caste families in her social circle simply didn't want to match her with their children. The ways in which caste continues to rear its ugly head in urban spaces is often overlooked, but it is something we need to talk about.

Hidden Stories of Empowerment: The Unsung Heroes

When we talk about empowerment, we often celebrate the well-known figures who have led the charge—Dr. Ambedkar, for instance, is a name that comes up in every conversation about caste and empowerment. But what about the grassroots leaders? What about those who never make the headlines but who change lives in ways that are just as profound?

Take the story of **Uma Devi**, a woman from a remote village in Tamil Nadu. Uma had no formal education, but she became a pioneer for women's rights and education in her community. She noticed that girls in her village were being denied education, not because they weren't capable, but because of the deep-rooted belief that education was "not for them." Uma didn't wait for anyone to help her; she took the matter into her own hands, starting a small school in her own home, encouraging parents to send their daughters to school. Her story is one of **quiet revolution**. No big government recognition, no international accolades—just a determined woman changing the lives of those around her, one child at a time.

Her work, though humble, has sparked a wave of transformation in her village. The girls who were once denied access to education are now graduating, becoming doctors, engineers, and teachers. They are empowered, not just through education, but through the breaking of old caste barriers. Uma's work reflects a truth: **real change doesn't always come from the top down**. It often comes from individuals who are willing to fight against the tide, who recognize the subtle forms of caste oppression and actively work to dismantle them.

Personal Reflection: A Call to Action

As we reflect on all of this, I want you to ask yourself—what kind of society do we want to build? One that recognizes that **progress isn't just about formal achievements**, but about creating a system where everyone can thrive. It's about breaking down barriers in both formal and informal sectors and acknowledging the real and invisible ways in which caste operates.

We need to continue to push for policies that support the economic upliftment of marginalized communities, but we also need to broaden the scope of what empowerment looks like. It's not just about quotas or reservations—it's about access to networks, resources, and opportunities that have historically been denied.

And perhaps most importantly, it's about **changing the conversation**. Caste discrimination is not just a relic of the past—it's a live issue that continues to shape our society in ways that are not always visible. We need to start recognizing that and actively work to dismantle the systems that perpetuate it.

So, next time you encounter a story of discrimination or hear about an act of exclusion, ask yourself: What's the story behind this? Is it simply about caste, or is it something deeper? Can we address the underlying system of exclusion? Let's keep these questions in mind, and let's start acting on them—every day, in every space we occupy.

The Persistent Shadow of Caste in Our Legal System

As we trace the threads of progress since the days of Ambedkar, it's impossible to ignore that caste-based discrimination still casts a long shadow over modern India. Sure, we have laws, even constitutional protections, but are they really enough? Are they truly being enforced? Let's take a closer look, not just at the laws themselves, but at the everyday stories of struggle that paint a far more nuanced picture of caste in the legal system.

Ambedkar, in his brilliance, didn't just focus on the historical realities of caste. He saw a future where the shackles of caste should be broken, where the promises of equality would finally ring true. But Ambedkar also understood something deeply crucial—laws alone aren't enough to change centuries of ingrained social hierarchies. And that's exactly where the modern Indian legal system is faltering.

The Law's Empty Promise

Take the *Untouchability Offences Act* or the *SC/ST Prevention of Atrocities Act,* for example. On paper, these are groundbreaking laws. They're supposed to protect the most marginalized in society, punishing anyone who dares to discriminate on the basis of caste. Yet, every time a Dalit person faces an atrocity—whether it's a brutal beating or a systematic denial of justice—the gap between what the law promises and what the law delivers becomes glaringly obvious.

Imagine this: A young Dalit man named Ravi, from a small village, is attacked by upper-caste men after allegedly drinking from the same well. He reports the assault to the police, only to be told that the "situation will resolve on its own" and that he "shouldn't stir up trouble." Ravi's case, much like countless others, goes ignored or dismissed. The perpetrators, who should face immediate legal repercussions under these laws, are instead left free to repeat their acts of violence without fear of accountability. Why? Because caste bias is not just an issue with the perpetrators; it's embedded deeply in the system.

The Slow Erosion of Justice

This brings us to another painful reality: the long delays in the judicial process. Ravi's case, if it even makes it to court, will likely take years to resolve. And even then, the chances of a just outcome are slim. Why? Caste bias in law enforcement and within the courts often leads to the marginalization of the voices of Dalit victims. The court may delay proceedings, ignore crucial evidence, or refuse to take action, because, let's face it, Dalit lives don't always matter in the same way to those who are supposed to uphold justice.

A friend of mine, someone who works tirelessly in the field of legal aid, once shared a powerful story about a case they were handling. A Dalit woman had been gang-raped by upper-caste men in her village. The woman's family, after being harassed by the police, finally managed to get her case to court. But the trial was delayed for over three years, only for the judge to deliver a half-hearted verdict that barely acknowledged the brutality of the crime. The system, which was designed to protect her, failed her at every turn.

Is There Hope for Change?

Now, before we drown in despair, let's take a moment to think about the possibilities that lie ahead. The current legal system has its deep flaws, but it doesn't mean we're bound to repeat the past. The first step toward real change is recognizing that the law can't work in a vacuum. It needs a cultural overhaul, a societal shift that calls for genuine empathy and respect for the oppressed.

Think of it this way: laws against caste-based discrimination are like the armor we wear, but what good is armor if the battlefield is still rigged against us? Our task is to make sure the system functions as it was meant to, and that means confronting biases within law enforcement, within the judiciary, and even within society at large. Imagine a scenario where the police aren't just trained to apply laws, but also to understand the deep-rooted histories of caste and oppression. Imagine a judiciary that doesn't just look at the letter of the law but understands the emotional and social reality behind each case.

What if the legal system became a tool for healing, not just punishment? What if we were to ensure swift trials, equipped with special fast-track courts to handle atrocities against marginalized communities? Imagine a world where victims like Ravi aren't just given a chance for justice—they're given the assurance that the law will protect them, immediately and effectively.

A Personal Touch to the Legal Struggle

I remember a time, not long ago, when I was speaking with a group of young activists. One of them, a woman from a Dalit background, shared how she had witnessed her family's struggle with a caste-based discrimination case that had taken nearly a decade to see any progress. For years, her family had been living with the knowledge that the accused, despite all the evidence against them, walked free, while they were forced to relive their trauma again and again. The frustration, anger, and helplessness in her voice were palpable.

But here's where I saw something beautiful: instead of sinking into despair, this young woman channeled her anger into action. She became a vocal advocate for reforming the judicial system and increasing accessibility for marginalized groups. Her story, painful as it was, became a catalyst for change—not just for her own community, but for countless others who had silently suffered in the shadows of an indifferent system.

It's people like her who give me hope. Despite the systemic failures, we still see a rise in grassroots movements pushing for accountability, for quicker trials, for more resources to support victims, and for a culture of justice that does not discriminate. These small victories are often overlooked, but they are no less significant in shifting the tides.

Conclusion: The Road Ahead

So, where do we go from here? We must first acknowledge that the legal system alone cannot dismantle caste-based oppression. However, a more sensitive, faster, and accountable legal system can serve as a foundation for long-term social change. The need for judicial reform is urgent, and that reform needs to be underpinned by a cultural transformation—a shift in how we, as a society, view caste and its pervasive impact.

We cannot afford to wait any longer for justice. It's time for us to make that change happen, not just with laws, but with our hearts, our minds, and our collective will. Because real justice isn't about waiting for the system to catch up—it's about making sure that the system catches up with us.

The Youth: Changing Attitudes Toward Caste and Social Transformation

In the sprawling, vibrant landscape of contemporary India, caste—a system that has shaped society for millennia—is gradually undergoing a transformation. The change is subtle but unmistakable. A generation of young people, born and raised amidst a rapidly evolving socio-economic environment, is beginning to challenge the long-standing norms that have defined caste-based identities. In this exploration, we delve into how India's youth perceive caste today, the ways in which they are dismantling its traditional hold, and whether the old system is truly fading or merely evolving.

The Changing Perception of Caste

The youth of today are arguably more educated, globally aware, and digitally connected than any previous generation. With access to information, a wider array of social influences, and opportunities for personal growth, many are more critical of caste-based discrimination than the generations before them. The traditional structures that once held caste rigidly in place—family expectations, social norms, and limited access to new ideas—are beginning to loosen their grip.

But is caste really fading, or is it merely being redefined?

Many young people now challenge caste as a social determinant of who they should be, what they can achieve, or whom they should marry. Caste-based attitudes that once permeated even the most personal of decisions—like career choices or relationships—are being questioned and actively contested. We are beginning to see this new perspective come to life through the actions of young individuals who are navigating the complexities of their identities with a desire for equality and justice.

For example, urban youth, who often interact with people from diverse backgrounds in their workplaces, educational institutions, and social spaces, are more likely to view caste through a lens of historical injustice rather than something that defines their present and future. In cities like Bangalore, Delhi, and Mumbai, it is no longer uncommon for young people to openly speak against caste-based discrimination or to question its relevance in modern India. The rise of social media platforms has further amplified these conversations, allowing young voices to challenge the status quo.

The Role of Social Media and Digital Activism

Social media has become a powerful tool for social change in the digital age, offering a platform for marginalized voices to rise above the noise of traditional media. This is especially significant for young people who are not only the primary users of social media platforms but also the driving force behind many social justice movements.

Take, for instance, the #DalitLivesMatter movement that gained momentum on platforms like Twitter and Instagram. Initiated by young Dalit activists, this movement uses the internet to bring attention to caste-based violence and discrimination. It gives voice to the oppressed, particularly young Dalits, and brings their stories of struggle to a global audience. Young people are utilizing hashtags, viral videos, and online campaigns to spread awareness, spark discussions, and push for policy changes. In the digital space, caste is being discussed and debated in ways that were previously unimaginable.

Digital activism isn't limited to just spreading awareness; it is actively transforming societal attitudes. One powerful example is how the youth have used memes and humor to challenge caste-related jokes or casual discrimination. Young Indians, especially those from privileged backgrounds, are now being exposed to the everyday realities of caste discrimination, and many are choosing to speak out in support of equality and justice.

Intercaste Marriages: The New Trend

One of the most powerful indicators of shifting attitudes toward caste is the growing trend of intercaste marriages among young people. Once seen as a social taboo, intercaste marriages are now increasingly viewed as a form of social rebellion—a way of rejecting centuries-old caste hierarchies. According to recent surveys, an increasing number of young people are choosing to marry outside their caste, reflecting a profound shift in values and priorities.

However, while intercaste marriages are on the rise, they remain a subject of great controversy, especially in rural areas and traditional families. For many, such marriages signify a break from the social order and a challenge to familial expectations. Yet, young people, especially those in urban areas, are beginning to see such unions as a natural extension of their belief in equality and individual agency. This shift is especially noticeable in well-educated, urban youth, who have the privilege of creating their own spaces and identities away from the gaze of older generations who still hold onto traditional caste values.

The rise of intercaste marriages, however, doesn't come without its challenges. Despite the increasing acceptance in cities, many young people still face societal and familial pressures to marry within their caste. It's a bitter irony that even while the younger generation strives for change, the older generation often remains steadfast in their belief that caste must be preserved. This contradiction between the younger and older generations is becoming increasingly evident.

The Generation Gap: Rural vs. Urban Divide

While young urbanites are challenging caste norms in bold new ways, this change is not universally shared across India. In rural areas, caste-based practices continue to play a dominant role in shaping people's lives, including their relationships, career prospects, and social interactions. Older generations in these communities often still adhere to caste-based hierarchies, seeing them as integral to the social fabric.

The older generation's deeply entrenched beliefs about caste clash with the ideals of the youth. In rural households, where caste-based discrimination continues to be a reality, young people often find themselves caught in a struggle between modernity and tradition. While urban youth may be able to embrace intercaste relationships and careers free from caste bias, young people in rural areas face resistance at home, at work, and in their communities when they attempt to break away from caste expectations.

One example of this tension is the challenge young people face when they try to pursue careers outside the caste-based expectations set by their families. A young person from a family of farmers might face resistance when choosing a career in technology or the arts, as these fields are often seen as "unsuitable" for someone from their caste. Despite this, more and more youth are pushing back against these boundaries, seeking careers that align with their interests and aspirations, even if they go against their family's wishes.

A Question That Resonates: Can a Common Person Achieve Success?

I'm reminded of a question that was once posed to me during a student meetup with law students in Chennai. A young man, eager to make his mark in the political world, asked me, "Can a common person achieve success?" It wasn't just a fleeting question for him; every time I saw him after that, he'd remind me to take note of it. His words lingered with me, especially as I watched him continue to pursue his dreams of entering politics. His question wasn't merely about ambition; it was about the very core of what it means to break free from the shackles of caste and social status.

For him, as for many others, the dream of success felt distant and sometimes out of reach, not just because of individual limitations but because of the system that quietly pushes people into predefined roles based on their caste, family background, or economic status. His question, though simple, echoed the frustration and determination of so many young people across India who are fighting to prove that success is not defined by the caste you're born into, but by the work you put in, the vision you hold, and the barriers you're willing to break.

Are Youth Truly Free from Caste?

While many of today's youth are breaking away from caste-based expectations, the question remains: **are they truly free from caste, or has caste simply been redefined?** The reality is complex. Even as young people embrace intercaste relationships, non-caste-based careers, and digital activism, caste continues to subtly shape their experiences. In fact, caste often operates in ways that are less overt but no less pervasive.

One of the significant factors at play is **the parental influence on how children are raised**. Many young people, especially those in rural areas, continue to grow up with deeply ingrained ideas about caste. Parents, even with the best intentions, often pass on these old attitudes—whether consciously or unconsciously. As children, they are taught, "We are more. We are not supposed to mingle with those from lower castes." These beliefs, though often hidden beneath layers of progressive education, can still have a subtle but significant impact on shaping the mindset of the younger generation.

This cycle of caste-based segregation doesn't just stay within the confines of the household. It extends into social circles, friendships, and even romantic relationships. Parents who hold these caste-based beliefs unwittingly pass them down, reinforcing the barriers that caste once imposed.

But here's the twist: **The rise of social media** has added a new layer to this issue. It's not just about the old-world parental influence anymore; today, caste identity is proudly showcased in the digital world. More and more young people are actively posting their caste names, colors, and identities on platforms like Instagram, Facebook, and Twitter. Some do it with pride, while others do it out of tradition or even to find a sense of belonging. It's become a norm in many social media spaces where caste identifiers are part of one's personal branding.

While some may argue this is a form of self-expression, it also perpetuates the idea of caste as an integral part of one's identity. It's almost like we are taking a step forward in terms of social change, but in the process, we're also taking two steps back. **What was once a hidden part of social identity is now out in the open, more visible than ever.**

This is where the contradiction lies. Youth today may declare themselves free from caste discrimination, but in practice, they may still be adhering to caste-based identities, especially when they find validation or comfort in it through their online presence. The digital world, where people are constantly trying to gain followers and likes, can sometimes inadvertently encourage individuals to cling to these identity markers as a way to connect with others who share the same background.

This digital caste consciousness creates a new form of social division, one that isn't as apparent in real-life interactions but becomes glaringly visible in the virtual space. Social media, which could have been an ally in challenging caste-based discrimination, has in many ways become a space where caste divides are perpetuated, even by the very generation that is claiming to reject them.

So, **are youth truly free from caste?** It's a question that doesn't have a clear-cut answer. While many young people reject the traditional constraints of caste and work hard to build a more egalitarian society, the subtlety with which caste continues to shape identities—both offline and online—suggests that freedom from caste is still a distant dream for many. The problem is not solely in how the youth think but also in the environment they are growing up in, where caste consciousness—passed down from one generation to the next—still plays a role in shaping attitudes and behaviors.

The struggle isn't just about changing individual mindsets; it's about addressing the systemic structures and inherited beliefs that keep caste alive, both in families and on social media. In this context, the youth may be free to challenge caste, but in many ways, they are also bound by it—just as much by the influence of their upbringing and the digital environment they inhabit as by the structures of society at large.

Conclusion: A New Dawn or a New Form of Caste?

In the end, the youth of India are undoubtedly pushing the boundaries of caste-based traditions. The growing trend of intercaste marriages, the influence of digital activism, and the rejection of caste-based career expectations all reflect a profound shift in values and attitudes. Yet, caste is not gone. It is merely evolving, taking on new forms that are less visible but still deeply influential.

So, are the youth truly free from caste? The answer is complex. While they are more aware and vocal in rejecting caste discrimination, it remains a powerful force in shaping their lives. The fight is far from over, but the youth's rebellion against the status quo is a sign of hope. The question now is whether this change will be enough to dismantle the deeply entrenched structures of caste or whether, over time, it will simply be redefined in ways that allow it to persist. What we do know is that the youth are no longer willing to accept caste as a permanent part of their identity—an act of resistance that is as necessary as it is urgent.

A New Vision for India's Future

As we stand at the crossroads of India's social evolution, one truth remains undeniable: caste-based inequality continues to haunt the fabric of our society, even as we strive toward progress. We've taken great strides in the legal realm—affirmative action, untouchability laws, and political representation have certainly made their mark. But to truly move forward, we need more than just legal victories or symbolic gestures. We need a shift—a transformation that is social, cultural, and deeply personal.

The fight against caste is not just about enacting laws or creating quotas; it's about changing hearts, minds, and ultimately, systems. Progress isn't just about numbers on a paper or the formal presence of marginalized groups in parliament or universities—it's about **real change** that touches every aspect of life. This means dismantling long-standing beliefs that some people are 'lesser' because of their birth. This means confronting uncomfortable truths about how caste continues to shape relationships, careers, and opportunities.

Now, let me take you back to a moment I mentioned earlier, I was speaking at a student meet-up in Chennai with law students, when one young, eager student asked me an unexpected question that has stuck with me ever since. "Can a common person, not born into power or privilege, truly succeed?" he asked, looking at me with a mix of curiosity and skepticism. The question wasn't just about success in the academic or political realms—it was deeper. It was about whether the shackles of caste, no matter how much we deny them, can ever truly be broken.

Every time I see that student now, he asks me the same thing: "So, have you found an answer?" To him, it's still a question that matters, and to me, it's a constant reminder that success in India, especially for those who don't fit the traditional mold, is still questioned, undermined, and even erased by the invisible weight of caste. And that's why, despite all the advances, the question of whether the 'common person'—someone not born into privilege—can truly succeed remains relevant today

I've noticed something unsettling: many young people today are proud to display their caste affiliations on social media, often even more openly than the generations before them. The digital age has allowed them to express themselves in ways previous generations could only dream of, but it has also given caste a new platform. It has become almost a badge of identity that some wear proudly. When I look at this, I'm reminded of a personal truth—**caste divides us before we even have a chance to understand one another**.

I also want to share a story that I find both heartbreaking and inspiring. A few years ago, I was talking to a friend who comes from a relatively privileged background. She had met someone from a lower caste and developed a connection. Initially, there was no problem—until they started facing judgment from her family. Her parents, who considered themselves modern and progressive, were shaken when they found out. They tried to convince her that caste didn't matter in her generation, but in their eyes, it still did. They tried to frame her relationship as "just a friendship," but it was clear to me—and to her—that caste was an invisible barrier she could never cross, not without serious consequences in her own family. In the end, the relationship broke down, and I couldn't help but feel how caste continues to interfere even in the most personal aspects of life.

Yet, at the same time, I see hope. I see young people fighting back against these ingrained divisions. **Intercaste marriages are on the rise**, albeit slowly, and young activists are using the very tools that divide us—social media—to bring awareness to caste-based issues. These efforts are not without their struggles, but they are a testament to the power of youth to challenge the status quo. **Youth-led movements** have started to focus on the importance of unity beyond caste, on building a future where relationships are based on shared humanity, not inherited hierarchy.

But there's something that still keeps me up at night. We speak about how caste might be fading in urban areas, how the city may represent a new world where caste becomes less visible. Yet, when I look deeper, I realize that caste is no longer overt. It is now subtle, ingrained in the networks of housing, hiring, and even marriage. In rural areas, it's still deeply entrenched. Caste violence continues, untouchability persists, and the social structure remains largely unchanged.

What this tells me is that **the fight against caste is not just about laws or digital platforms; it is about a complete cultural shift**. It's about educating the next generation to not just question caste but to refuse to let it define them. We need to focus on **creating systems that foster**

equality at every level—from the smallest village to the bustling city. It's about making sure that opportunities are not just available to a select few, but accessible to everyone, regardless of where they come from or what they are born into.

So, how do we move forward? **Social transformation** must be at the core of any solution. We need to continue building on the progress made through affirmative action and ensure its proper implementation. But we also need to **shift the cultural narrative**. A society where caste is not a barrier to education, success, or social acceptance must be our collective goal. It's time to stop seeing caste as a problem for others to solve and start viewing it as our own problem to overcome.

A New India

In the future I dream of, caste is not just absent from policy; it's absent from **people's minds and hearts**. We live in a society where every individual is judged not by the history of their ancestors but by their talents, character, and contributions. The real work begins when we stop asking, "How much progress have we made?" and start asking, "What can we do today to ensure that everyone, regardless of caste, has the same opportunities to live with dignity?"

In the end, true change comes not from laws alone, but from **a collective, conscious effort**—a shift in how we raise our children, how we treat those around us, and how we see each other. The future of India depends on us: the young, the old, the privileged, the marginalized. We have the power to make this vision of equality a reality, but we must choose to act.

Let's work toward that future together. **Not as caste-based identities, but as citizens of a just, inclusive India.**

WHAT WILL BE INDIA'S FUTURE AND WHAT SHOULD BE

> *"True change begins not in laws or speeches, but in the quiet awakening of every mind that chooses to see all souls as equal."*

India stands at a crucial juncture, where its past, present, and future intersect in a complex web of progress and challenges. As the world's largest democracy, India holds immense potential to become a global leader in economy, technology, and social justice. But let's pause here for a moment—potential alone is not enough. The future is not a given; it is a choice. It is the sum of our decisions, our struggles, and most importantly, our willingness to change what must be changed.

But what does change really mean? It is not about small adjustments or surface-level reforms—it is about dismantling deep-rooted inequalities, rethinking what progress truly stands for, and ensuring that no one is left behind in our pursuit of growth. If we continue to walk the same path without questioning its flaws, we will only reinforce the cycles of exclusion and injustice that have plagued our history. The India of tomorrow will not be defined by its past achievements but by its courage to demand better, to reject complacency, and to build a future where justice is not conditional but absolute.

The Future We Are Headed Towards: A Mixed Reality

If we simply let things be, what kind of India are we looking at in the coming decades? A country with soaring GDP numbers yet deepening inequalities? A nation-leading in artificial intelligence but failing in basic human rights? A democracy on paper but shackled by communal and caste politics? The truth is that growth without justice is hollow, and justice without action is just a word.

Economists and political analysts predict a future where India becomes the third-largest economy in the world. Technological advancements, urbanization, and digital revolutions will push us forward. But beneath these dazzling projections lies a darker reality—climate crises, widening economic disparity, and increasing ideological polarization. Will we be a nation of progress, or will we simply perfect the art of oppression in a digital age?

A Story of Two Indias

Let me tell you a story, so that you get a recap of all the layers of inequality that still define our nation, Two young men—let's call them Raju and Arjun—are born in the same country, but in two different Indias. Raju, born in a marginalized community, grows up in a village where schools exist, but teachers rarely show up. His parents work as laborers, and no matter how hard he studies, opportunities seem out of reach. Arjun, on the other hand, is born into a family of privilege. He has access to elite schools, connections, and resources. When both of them apply for the same job, Arjun walks in with confidence, knowing his father's friend owns the company. Raju walks in with hope, carrying the weight of generations who never made it past primary school.

Who gets the job?

Now, I am not saying Arjun is at fault for being born privileged. But the system that decides their fate is. If we continue down this path, India will not be a land of dreams—it will be a land where dreams are assigned based on where you were born. This is the future we must change.

The Future India Deserves: A Vision for Progress

So, what should India's future look like? Not just a country of economic superpowers, but a land where justice is not an afterthought. A country where people don't have to fight for basic rights but are empowered to dream beyond survival. A nation where caste and class do not dictate destiny. Here's how we build it:

1. Justice, Not Just Development

Let's begin with the fundamental pillar of progress: justice. Economic growth cannot be measured in skyscrapers while people at the bottom still struggle for survival. Justice is not an accessory to progress; it is the foundation. Policies should not just aim to increase jobs but ensure that dignity and fairness are embedded in every opportunity. No Raju should have to work twice as hard to get half the chances Arjun takes for granted. True development is when privilege no longer dictates destiny.

And justice is not just about economics—it is about humanity. What does it say about a nation that sends satellites into space yet allows manual scavenging to persist? That builds world-class universities but forces Dalit students to drop out due to systemic discrimination? We cannot call ourselves a progressive society while tolerating these injustices. If we want real change, we must redefine what we call "development."

Development without justice is a hollow promise. The measure of a nation's progress is not in its GDP but in the dignity of its people. It is time we stopped celebrating economic milestones while ignoring the millions left behind. The future of India cannot just be built on numbers—it must be built on justice, equity, and the unwavering belief that no one should be left behind.

Economic growth cannot be measured in skyscrapers while people at the bottom still struggle for survival. Justice means policies that don't just create jobs but ensure fair wages and opportunities. No Raju should have to work twice as hard to get half the chances Arjun takes for granted. True development is when privilege is no longer an advantage.

And justice is not just about economics—it's about dignity. A future where manual scavengers still exist is not progress. A future where Dalit students drop out because they are bullied in classrooms is not a success. If we want real change, we must redefine what we call "development."

2. Democracy That Works for the People

A real democracy is not just about elections—it is about representation, accountability, and action. We often hear about the numbers—how many people voted, how many seats a party won, and so on. But what if these numbers don't tell us the full story? What if democracy isn't just a matter of casting votes and choosing leaders, but about ensuring that the chosen leaders serve the people with transparency and integrity?

Electoral reforms must go beyond fixing the machinery of voting. We need to uproot the weeds of money-driven politics that pollute the very idea of democratic representation. When elections are influenced by wealth and power, the will of the people becomes secondary to the interests of a few. Governance must be rooted in transparency, where every action taken by those in power is open for scrutiny. Leaders must be held accountable, not only during election years but every single day of their tenure. If democracy does not translate into dignity for every citizen, it is merely a performance, not a true system of governance.

Now, pause for a moment and imagine: What would it look like if Parliament actually reflected the diverse voices of the people, rather than the corporate interests that often pull the strings behind the scenes? What if government policies were crafted with the public's welfare in mind, not the pursuit of votes or the appeasement of powerful lobbies? This is the kind of democracy we need to build.

But this isn't an easy task. It requires a shift in mindset, not just at the top but across the entire society. We need to demand more from our leaders—more than empty promises, more than political theater. We need a democracy that demands that our leaders engage with us not just when they need votes, but in the daily conversations that define the life of the nation.

True democracy is built on the understanding that every citizen's voice matters—not just during election time, but all year round. It means creating a system where decisions aren't made behind closed doors or based on power structures that do not reflect the diversity of the people. We must move beyond seeing democracy as a transaction—where politicians give us what we want only to take something back when they need it. We must see it as a continuous relationship of respect, accountability, and action.

A system where public policies don't just serve the privileged few but uplift those who have long been silenced and ignored. A democracy where the poor, the marginalized, the oppressed—everyone—can look at the government and feel it serves them, not in part, but in its entirety. This isn't just an ideal; this is the standard we must hold ourselves to. Because a democracy that only works for a select few is not democracy at all—it is a charade

3. A Society Beyond Caste and Communal Divisions

Ambedkar didn't just critique the caste system; he saw its long-term consequences and the deep psychological scars it inflicted upon society. Today, caste operates much like a silent undercurrent. It may not be as overt as it once was, but it still shapes everything—from the opportunities we receive to the relationships we form. The reality we have to accept is that casteism doesn't always announce itself in bold colors. It often wears a mask of respectability, hiding beneath the surface of seemingly harmless words and actions.

But here's where we need to look inward: *Are we complicit in this?* Not just in big, obvious ways, but in the subtle, seemingly insignificant moments of our lives? The quiet biases we carry, the assumptions we make about others based on their background, their community, or their social standing? It's these invisible patterns, these ingrained habits, that perpetuate caste-based distinctions.

Consider this: How often do you make the effort to truly see people for who they are, beyond their caste or social identity? We're all guilty of unknowingly carrying around biases we were never taught to challenge. But the question is, when are we going to stop and say, "Enough"? When will we stop allowing caste, in all its forms, to dictate how we see ourselves and others? When will we reject it—fully, consciously, and unapologetically?

The change we need doesn't come from a place of guilt or obligation—it comes from a place of active, intentional rethinking. It's about noticing the small, everyday moments: the person you decide to invite into your circle, the language you use without even thinking about it, the people you choose to stand up for when they're being sidelined, the spaces you create where all are welcome. This is where the real transformation happens—not on grand stages or in political speeches, but in the small, mundane actions we take every single day.

As Ambedkar said, the Constitution alone cannot free us. It is our mindset that needs to evolve. And that evolution starts with each of us, questioning not only the system but ourselves. It's about asking the difficult questions: *What have I inherited? What do I need to unlearn? How can I actively dismantle the systems of inequality I've been part of, even unknowingly?* It's a journey of constant self-reflection, of holding ourselves accountable, and of making sure our actions align with our ideals.

True change is rooted in this daily commitment to reshaping the world—not through theoretical debates, but through the living, breathing actions we take in the real world. So, the next time you find yourself in a room with others, ask yourself: *Who is missing from this room?* and *What can I do to make this space truly inclusive?*

4. Education: The Great Equalizer

Imagine an India where every child, regardless of their caste, community, or socioeconomic status, is given access to the same high-quality education. A place where knowledge isn't defined by the birthright of your family but by the power of your own mind. In this ideal world, it's not your lineage that determines your future, but the quality of education you receive and the opportunities you're given. Education is often touted as the "great equalizer," but how many of us have truly seen it live up to its promise?

We live in a society where privilege often dictates success. The best schools, the best teachers, the most enriched environments—all are confined to the children of the wealthy and the powerful. And then there are others—the ones born into communities that have been historically excluded—whose potential is wasted simply because they don't have the resources. But what if we could break that cycle?

We need to rethink education—not as a luxury reserved for a select few, but as a fundamental right for all. It isn't just about textbooks and classrooms. It's about creating an ecosystem where every child can grow, thrive, and rise beyond the circumstances they were born into. It's about giving every child access to the same opportunities—the kind that build character, nurture dreams, and empower them to break free from the shackles of societal divisions.

The truth is, investing in education isn't just an act of charity—it's essential for the survival of any nation that dares to dream of greatness. A country's potential is only as strong as its youngest minds. And if we're going to truly rise, we have to stop thinking about education as a distant privilege and start viewing it as the foundation for a better future.

Consider this: What does it say about us as a society if the only children who receive the best education are those who can afford it? If a child's birth determines their access to opportunities, then how are we to claim we live in a democracy of equal chance? Our educational institutions must be more than mere buildings; they must be sanctuaries of hope, promising every child a future where their potential is what determines their destiny—not their caste, creed, or class.

We don't just need reforms; we need a revolution. A revolution where the idea of privilege no longer holds sway over opportunity. A revolution where the playing field is leveled, and children from all walks of life can walk into a classroom and feel they belong.

This isn't about charity. This is about survival. The survival of a nation that will not stand still, but one that is committed to reaching the fullest potential of its people. A nation where every child, regardless of their background, can dream big and make that dream a reality.

So, let's ask ourselves: Are we willing to invest in the future of our children? Are we ready to create an education system that belongs to everyone—not just the privileged few? Because the truth is, a country that fails its children—by denying them the education they deserve—ultimately fails itself. And, to break free from this cycle, we need to start by giving every child the one thing that no one can take away: the power of knowledge.

5. Sustainability: A Future Worth Living In

What good is a thriving economy if we cannot breathe its air or drink its water? This isn't a rhetorical question—it's one that demands our attention, now more than ever. Climate change has moved from a distant concept in textbooks to something we experience daily. It's flooding our cities, choking our rivers, burning our crops, and threatening our very survival. The truth is, we've reached a point where the question isn't just about saving the environment; it's about saving ourselves.

Think about it: how many of us have stopped to consider the consequences of the choices we make every day? Whether it's the plastic bottle we toss away or the emissions we release into the air without a second thought, we're all complicit. It's easy to feel disconnected, to think that our individual actions don't matter in the grand scheme of things. But here's the reality: small drops make an ocean. It's the collective weight of our choices that will either sink us or save us.

So, why are we still clinging to outdated practices that only feed the destruction around us? Why are we still choosing convenience over sustainability? We need to challenge the very systems that allow this cycle to continue. If we continue on the path we're on, the next generation won't be fighting for progress—they will be fighting for survival. They won't be inheriting a world full of opportunities—they'll inherit a world ravaged by choices we failed to make.

Here's where we need to change the narrative: the economy we strive for can and must coexist with nature. We must invest in renewable energy, not as a "trend," but as an essential part of our future. Solar, wind, and hydropower are no longer options—they are imperatives. Sustainable farming practices, eco-friendly industries, and waste management need to become the backbone of our economy. We cannot afford to think short-term, as we've done for decades. What we do today will echo through generations.

But here's the real kicker: sustainability isn't just about the planet—it's about people. It's about ensuring that the poorest, who are most vulnerable to climate change, have the resources they need to not just survive but thrive. It's about creating a future that doesn't just work for the privileged few but for all of us, equally. And that's something worth fighting for.

If we are to truly evolve as a society, we must learn that progress doesn't mean endless growth at the cost of our natural resources. True progress is sustainable progress. True growth doesn't deplete—it replenishes. If we don't start thinking like this, we might very well be the last generation to enjoy the comforts of a habitable planet.

Let's face it: this isn't just a political issue or a social one—it's a survival issue. Our climate isn't waiting for us to catch up. The sooner we begin, the sooner we create an India where future generations don't have to fight for survival, but can instead work towards progress. Let's take responsibility. Let's act now.

6. Technology That Serves the Many, Not Just the Few

The digital revolution should not deepen existing inequalities. As we enter an era where the internet, AI, and automation are reshaping the world, these technologies must be tools for empowerment, not exclusion. The promise of technology is to bring people together, to open doors that were once closed, and to offer opportunities that can level the playing field for all. But if access to these technologies is restricted to only the privileged, if only certain groups benefit from their potential, then we are not witnessing a revolution—we are perpetuating a new form of inequality, a digital caste system.

Imagine a world where technology works for everyone: where no one is left behind because they lack access to the internet, or cannot afford the latest devices. Where the development of AI and automation leads to more inclusive workplaces, where people of all backgrounds can find meaningful work. This is not a distant dream, but a future we can create, provided we ensure that policies are in place to make technology accessible, affordable, and understandable for all.

Policymakers must prioritize digital literacy alongside traditional education, ensuring that all individuals, regardless of socioeconomic status, have the skills and knowledge to thrive in an increasingly digital world. This is about more than just giving people access to a device—it's about creating a society where everyone has the opportunity to unlock the potential of technology, to contribute to it, and to benefit from it.

Without these measures, we risk entrenching divisions in society, where those with access to cutting-edge technology hold the keys to success, while those without are left to struggle, marginalized by the very tools that are meant to advance us. The digital revolution must be for all, not just the few.

7. Gender Equality Beyond Slogans: A Call for True Inclusivity

We've heard it all before, haven't we? "Women need empowerment." But let's pause and think: What if the real issue isn't about giving women something they lack, but rather, giving them what's rightfully theirs—equal footing? Empowerment sounds like a favor, a gesture of charity, a concept that implies women are somehow incomplete without it. But the truth is, women—and indeed, all gender identities—do not need to be "empowered"; they need to be treated as equals in every space—whether it's in boardrooms, classrooms, political offices, or at home.

We need to move beyond the language of "empowerment" and start talking about what people are owed—respect, safety, financial independence, and leadership. These are not privileges; these are rights. When we talk about equality, we often focus on the immediate needs—protection from violence, access to education, healthcare, or fair wages. But if we truly want progress, we need to start with the bigger picture: leadership. People should not only be allowed to participate in the decisions that shape our world; they should be the ones leading these conversations. A future where anyone, regardless of gender identity, is merely "allowed" to occupy space isn't enough. We need a future where they shape it, where they are the architects of their destiny.

Beyond Women: A Call for Respect and Equality for All

The conversation around gender equality often revolves around cisgender women, but it's important that we move beyond that. Gender equality should not be limited to just one group; it must extend to everyone, including those who may not fit into the conventional categories of male or female. Transgender, non-binary, and gender-fluid individuals have historically faced exclusion and oppression. But even more so, they, like everyone else, deserve to live in a world where they are treated with respect and dignity, no matter how they identify.

Even if their identity or life choices don't align with your personal beliefs, the least we can do is respect them as human beings. It's not our place to judge or belittle others based on their identity. We don't have to fully understand or agree with someone's gender identity, but we can still show basic human respect. After all, what truly matters is how we treat one another. In a world where people feel free to express themselves, no one should feel less than, simply because they are different.

Creating Safe Spaces for All

Safety isn't just about avoiding physical harm; it's about creating environments where everyone feels valued and secure. Yet, in many places, women, trans individuals, and non-binary people continue to experience violence, discrimination, and exclusion. This doesn't happen because of who they are—it happens because society refuses to let go of outdated norms and ideals that limit the potential of all individuals.

We have a responsibility to make spaces safer for everyone. True safety doesn't come from enforcing strict gender roles or policing people's behavior. It comes from fostering a culture where all individuals are protected, respected, and allowed to exist freely. Whether you're a cisgender woman, a transgender person, or anyone who doesn't conform to traditional gender norms, you deserve to live without fear of being harmed or discriminated against.

Financial Independence and Leadership: A Right for Everyone

Financial independence is often a key to freedom. It allows individuals, regardless of gender identity, to control their own lives and decisions. No one should be dependent on anyone else for their livelihood, for their voice, or for their future. Financial independence means that a person can be their own advocate, make their own decisions, and lead without restraint.

But this can't happen if people are continually held back by stereotypes or discrimination based on their gender identity. For true progress, we need leadership that is reflective of the diverse society we live in. Whether you are a woman, trans person, non-binary individual, or anyone else, your voice is just as valuable and your leadership just as important.

A Future of Equality for All

So, what does a future of equality look like? It's a world where everyone—regardless of gender—can live without fear of discrimination, where all people are treated with the respect they deserve. A world where no one has to apologize for who they are or how they express themselves. Whether you identify as a woman, a man, or anything beyond or in between, you should be able to walk through the world with dignity.

This future isn't just a distant dream—it can be a reality if we commit to respecting one another and recognizing the humanity in everyone, no matter how different their identity or experiences may be from our own. Respecting someone, even if you don't fully understand or agree with them, is the first step in creating a world where everyone has the opportunity to thrive. And that's something we all deserve.

A Future We Must Demand

We live in a world where labels are placed on people based on their gender, caste, religion, or where they were born. These labels often dictate the opportunities available to them, shaping their futures before they even get a chance to decide who they want to be. But here's the thing: equality doesn't mean treating everyone the same. It means giving everyone the resources and opportunities they need to thrive.

When we talk about social justice, it's about recognizing that not everyone is starting the race at the same spot. For some, the path ahead is smooth and well-lit; for others, it's a long, dark road, filled with obstacles they didn't create. So, equality isn't just about giving everyone the same thing—it's about ensuring that everyone has what they need to succeed, no matter where they come from or who they are.

Think about the word *unity*. It's often misunderstood. Unity doesn't mean uniformity. It doesn't mean that we all have to think the same, act the same, or have the same life experiences. True unity comes from recognizing and celebrating our differences. It's about finding strength in diversity. Unity is about bringing people together, not by asking them to erase what makes them unique, but by acknowledging those differences and making room for them.

Humanity is, at its core, the recognition that we are all connected. We all share this world. We all breathe the same air, live under the same sky, and are bound by the same dreams of a better life. If we forget that, we lose our sense of shared responsibility. The struggles of one are the struggles of all. And so, if we're serious about humanity, we must be serious about equality—about making sure that no one is left behind simply because of who they are or where they come from.

This leads us to social justice. Social justice isn't just a lofty ideal; it's a call to action. It's a commitment to creating systems that ensure everyone has the opportunity to thrive. It's about recognizing that privilege exists and actively working to level the playing field for those who have been historically marginalized. It's about dismantling the barriers that keep people trapped in cycles of poverty, discrimination, and exclusion.

But here's the hard truth: Social justice doesn't happen by itself. It requires all of us—each and every one of us—to show up. To challenge our own biases, to question systems that perpetuate inequality, and to stand in solidarity with those whose voices are often silenced. It requires us to respect the humanity in others, even when their lives and experiences differ from our own.

And this respect goes beyond just tolerance—it's about true acceptance. Even if something doesn't fit within your belief system, even if it doesn't feel "right" to you personally, we must still respect others. Respect isn't about agreement; it's about recognizing the dignity and worth of every human being. This is where real unity begins.

So, let's be clear about this: A future that truly represents us all can only be built on a foundation of respect, equality, and justice. It won't happen overnight, and it won't happen if we don't each do our part. But every small action matters—whether it's standing up for someone who's being treated unfairly, questioning the systems around us, or simply respecting the humanity in someone who might seem different from you.

The future we demand is one where we don't just co-exist, but where we genuinely thrive together. It's a future where every individual is valued for who they are, not what they're expected to be. It's a future where unity is rooted in the acceptance of our differences and where equality isn't just a dream, but a reality for all.

INDIA HAS A WHOLE

> All are equal.
> Not because we pretend they are.
> But because they always were.

No one is born to rule. No one is born to kneel.

Caste is not a divine truth. It is a man-made myth—one that has lingered like smoke in the air we breathe. A myth that has dictated dreams, clipped wings, and handed out lives like roles in a script no one agreed to.

And yet, some still ask: "Is caste still relevant?"

We ask back:
When a child is denied admission because of their surname, when a topper's name is erased from the honors list, when a groom is killed for loving beyond her 'place'—do you really need a reminder that caste is alive?

This is not a call to the streets.
This is a call to our minds. To our mirrors. To the quiet conversations we have with ourselves.

It begins in how we see the world.
It begins in how we see each other.

It begins in how we see ourselves.

And maybe it begins best in the words of Thiruvalluvar:

> **"Pirapokkum ella uyirkum"**
> *Birth is common to all beings.*

So, if birth is equal, then who divided us after?

This is the fundamental question of this book. Who divided us, and why do we still carry those lines like scars we're too afraid to heal?

This book is not just a compilation of arguments. It is a journey—through history, policy, power, and people. It is born out of anger, yes, but also out of love. Love for a country that was never meant to be a monolith. Love for a Constitution that dared to dream of equality. Love for all the voices that go unheard in the noise of mainstream narratives.

In the course of finishing this book, I found myself unable to turn away from the burning realities of today—the questions that echo in every corner of this country. Questions about **caste**, **language**, **identity**, and the **future of representation**.

Before We Move Forward...

As I neared the end of this book—pen in hand, heart full of questions—I couldn't walk away without turning to the winds blowing through our present. I began with the past, yes. But in tracing caste through centuries, I found myself staring straight at today. And today demands a pause.

In the pulse of our politics, in the hush of our classrooms, in the languages slipping quietly from lips—we are witnessing a shift. One that may redefine what India stands for.

How could I not speak of it?

The **Caste Census**, the **Delimitation debate**, the **Three-Language Policy**—these are not just policy proposals. They are reflections of who we are willing to count, whose voices we choose to amplify, and whose stories we let fade into silence.

This wasn't part of the plan when I started.

But some truths *ask* to be written.

And some questions refuse to wait for a later chapter.

So before we draw conclusions, let's step into these urgent questions—*not just as observers, but as citizens, as voices, as dreamers of a more just tomorrow.*

Delimitation: Fair Political Power or Mathematical Injustice?

What happens when democracy becomes a numbers game? The idea behind delimitation is to ensure equal representation by adjusting electoral boundaries based on population. Fair enough, right?

But here's the catch: while the Constitution intended for balance, political motivations have tilted the scale. For decades, southern states worked hard to control population growth, investing in health and education. Now, they are being punished for it.

The frozen 1971 census is set to thaw. If delimitation proceeds with future censuses, power will shift toward the populous north. Representation in Parliament will tilt dramatically, marginalizing states that have actually followed national policy.

Is this justice? Or is it a betrayal wrapped in statistics?

In the name of "equality," we risk erasing the voices of entire regions. Development is becoming a disadvantage. Governance that was meant to be rewarded is now a reason for political sidelining.

Delimitation must be discussed. Not in hushed tones, but loudly, boldly, with clarity. Because true representation is not just about headcounts—it's about history, effort, and the soul of federalism.

Caste Census & Sensitivity: Counting Our Inequalities So No One Is Invisible

For too long, caste has been both everywhere and nowhere.

Everywhere in lived experience. Nowhere in data.

We talk of social justice, of upliftment, of equality. But how can we address what we refuse to count? How can we claim to dismantle caste-based barriers when we don't even know the scale of those walls?

A caste census is not about dividing the country. It's about finally seeing it—*all* of it. Not just the elite. Not just the privileged. But the many who build our homes, cook our food, clean our roads, and still fight for dignity.

Opponents call it regressive. They say it will bring caste back into the mainstream.

But ask yourself: *Did caste ever leave?*

This isn't about creating new divisions. It's about recognising old wounds. Only when we know who is where—in education, in jobs, in healthcare—can we truly begin to speak of equity.

Numbers don't lie. But silence does.

Three-Language Policy: Unity or Silent Erasure of Regional Souls?

Every coin has two sides, and the story of India is no different. One side gleams with the brilliance of our diversity—our many languages, cultures, religions, and festivals, all of which make us unique in the world.No other country has embraced such complexity with such tenacity. But in this pursuit of unity, let us not lose the very voices that make us whole.

I want you to think for a moment about this diversity. The multitude of languages spoken, the varied cultures celebrated, the many religions coexisting in what should be a harmonious union. This is what makes India, India. This is our identity.

And yet, what are we doing with it?

Now think about the three-language policy. At first glance, it seems harmless—even well-intentioned. Learn one more language, they say. What could be wrong with that?

But ask: Is this really about adding something new? Or is it about replacing something old?

They say, "Just one more language." But history has shown us that it never stops at one. The minute we begin placing one language above others, we start erasing the rest. It begins subtly—schools prioritizing it, jobs requiring it, public discourse shifting. And then, without realizing, the language of the people becomes informal, less valued, and slowly fades.

This is how cultural erasure works. It whispers. It shifts. And then one day, it silences.

Look at Bombay. Once a city where Marathi thrived, now struggling to find its voice amidst the dominance of Hindi. Similar stories echo across Tamil Nadu, Karnataka, Kerala, and beyond.

So no, it's not just about an extra subject in school. It's about identity, dignity, and the right to belong on our own terms. When the government enforces a singular linguistic identity, it isn't shaping communication. It is reshaping thought.

Unity must never come at the cost of uniqueness. **But here lies the central question:** Is unity through uniformity real unity—or just quiet domination? Unity that forces cultural conformity and linguistic hegemony risks alienating the very people it is supposed to unite. True unity, perhaps, is built on diversity and respect for the multiplicity of identities that exist across India. It is crucial to recognize that language is a symbol of power, and the struggle for linguistic rights is, in many ways, the struggle for equality.

Intersectionality

Caste is never a standalone force. It is deeply intertwined with gender, region, religion, and class, each layer amplifying the oppression faced by individuals. Take, for instance, a Dalit woman in Bihar—her caste condemns her to a life of systemic marginalization, but her gender subjects her to an added dimension of violence and invisibility. The double burden of caste and patriarchy crushes her at every step. Now contrast this with a dominant-caste man in Tamil Nadu, whose access to education, opportunity, and social status is largely unchallenged—an embodiment of privilege, shaped not just by caste, but by region. Caste also plays a unique role when combined with religion; a Dalit Muslim faces a distinct form of exclusion, where both his religious and caste identity mark him as inferior, compared to a Dalit Hindu. This intersectionality isn't just a theory—it's the lived reality for millions, showing us that caste isn't just about social ranking; it's about how every identity marker compounds and reinforces the other. When we talk about caste, we cannot ignore the complex web of identities that each individual must navigate, where power isn't just distributed by caste alone, but through a mosaic of intertwined forces.

Reinforcing Constitutional Ideals

The Constitution of India promises justice, liberty, equality, and fraternity to all its citizens, irrespective of caste, gender, religion, or region. Yet, when we examine the policies and practices that continue to shape our nation—be it through the delimitation process, the caste census, or the imposition of a singular language—one cannot help but ask: *Are we truly living the Constitution we were promised?*

The ideals enshrined in the Preamble were meant to form the foundation of a just and equitable society. But today, as we confront the realities of caste-based politics, linguistic imposition, and regional disparities, we must reflect: *Has our Constitution become a mere aspirational document, or are we living its promises every day?*

It's time we ask ourselves if we're upholding the Constitution in its fullest form—or if we've allowed it to bend and break under the weight of political interests and historical injustices.

We Must Not Forget...

India is not a monolith. It was never meant to be. And the truth is, it *never has been*. We are a land born from contradictions and coexistence, from debate and dissent, from kings and rebels, from poets and revolutionaries. This conclusion is not just the end of a book—it is a return to where we began: to the heartbeat of this nation, pulsing with the dreams of those who came before us, and the demands of those who walk beside us.

Our Constitution—so often quoted, yet so rarely understood in its spirit—wasn't built to suppress difference. It was drafted in the ashes of Partition, in the cries of freedom, and in the hope that no Indian would be invisible again. It gave us the promise of dignity, not merely existence. It gave us rights, not just rules. But somewhere along the way, that promise has been bruised.

We've walked through the shadows in these pages—the legacy of caste that continues to haunt our politics, the erasure of language and culture through top-down policies, the ghosts of colonial divisions rebranded in democratic rhetoric. We've unpacked the uneasy truths behind electoral politics and caste calculations, behind representation and tokenism, behind regional neglect and forced homogeneity.

We spoke of the leaders who stood up, and those who were shut down. We saw Thiruvalluvar reminding us that all lives have equal worth. We traced the journey of caste not just as a social order but as a political tool. We questioned whether our democracy uplifts or merely manages. We looked at the Constitution with reverence, but also with righteous rage.

We asked the hardest question: who divided us—and who continues to benefit from those divisions?

And now, as we close these pages, I ask one more: What kind of India do *you* want to live in?

Will it be one where policies are measured by how many they exclude, or by how much they empower? Will it be one where a Dalit child dreams without fear of violence, where a tribal village speaks its tongue with pride, where a woman's worth is not debated in Parliament but defended in practice? Will it be one where the line on a map doesn't decide your access to justice, to education, to dignity?

Because caste still kills. Language still isolates. Region still marginalizes. And we must stop pretending otherwise.

This is not a call to nostalgia. I am not asking you to return to some imagined golden past. I am asking you to move forward—with clarity and courage.

What we need now is not mere resistance—it is reclamation. Reclaiming what it means to be Indian. Reclaiming politics as a tool of service, not spectacle. Reclaiming leadership as duty, not dynasty. Reclaiming justice as everyday action, not court orders. Reclaiming the Constitution as a living document—not a museum relic, but a mirror we must hold to ourselves."

And if we do not, we risk losing the very thing that makes us Indian—not our skin, our food, our flags—but our plurality. That delicate, defiant, dazzling plurality that says: I am because we all are.

In this book, I chose not to shy away from pain. Because pain tells the truth. But I also chose hope. Because hope dares to change the truth. We've seen the paradox of representation—how it can liberate and limit. We've felt the need for a caste census—not to divide further, but to see clearly. We've asked what justice really looks like, in a country that has learned to tolerate inequality by hiding it behind numbers.

I wrote about delimitation not because it's trendy, but because it threatens the very idea of equal political power. I wrote about the three-language policy not to inflame, but to protect the soul of regional identity. These are not academic footnotes. These are lived realities. And ignoring them is a privilege this country can no longer afford.

The road ahead is not easy. It never was. But history has never bowed to the timid. It listens to those who persist.

So let's persist.

Let us fight not against each other, but for each other. Let us fight not for dominance, but for dignity. Let us build an India where every voice matters—where no child is told their name is too low, their language too local, their dream too much.

Because in the end, India belongs to all of us—or it belongs to none at all.

AUTHOR'S TAKEAWAY

Now that this book is complete, what lingers in my mind is a question to you. Perhaps what should remain is my opinion — but before I share that, it is worth speaking of the journey this book has taken after its final page was written.

It was not an easy road. The manuscript travelled to many hands — leaders, writers, students. With each person I met, the first question was almost always the same: "What is this book about?" A natural question, yes, but what struck me most was their reaction after hearing my answer.

I would say, "It speaks of India's socio-political reality, of how caste continues to shape our society, and why it must be buried." And their reply — "That's not possible."

Hearing that from ordinary people might not surprise me. But to hear it from those who have fought in this path for years — that was deeply saddening. Yet, it is the reality we face.

Still, I stand here, grateful. Grateful for the unwavering support given to both this book and to me by so many. And now, my opinion — the simplest answer I can give to a complicated question:

When each and every human places humanity first, and truly accepts that all are equal, only then will the promise of equality stop being just words on paper — and become the way we live.

Because the day we stop asking "Who are you?" and start asking "How are you?" will be the day we finally become the nation we dream to be.

BIBLIOGRAPHY

Books & Academic Works:

- Ambedkar, B. R. (1923). *The Problem of the Rupee: Its Origin and Its Solution*. P. S. King & Son.
- Ambedkar, B. R. (1936). *Annihilation of Caste*. Self-published.
- Ambedkar, B. R. (1946). *Who Were the Shudras?* Thacker & Co.
- Ambedkar, B. R. (1955). *Thoughts on Linguistic States*. Government of India.
- Ambedkar, B. R. (1957). *The Buddha and His Dhamma*. Siddharth College Publications. *(Published posthumously)*
- Desai, A. R. (1990). *Politics of Caste in Post-Independence India*. Popular Prakashan.
- Gandhi, M. K. (1909). *Hind Swaraj or Indian Home Rule*. Navajivan Publishing House.
- Gandhi, M. K. (1941). *Constructive Programme: Its Meaning and Place*. Navajivan Publishing House.
- Gandhi, M. K. (Autobiography). *The Story of My Experiments with Truth*. Navajivan Publishing House.
- Kalyanasundaram, V. (n.d.). *Thirukkural: A Universal Code of Ethics*. [Publication details needed].
- Puri, S. K. (n.d.). *Caste and Democracy in India*. [Publication info needed].
- Thiruvalluvar. *Thirukkural*. Various editions

🗎 Journals and Scholarly Articles:

- Brass, P. R. (1994). Caste and Electoral Politics in India. *The Journal of Asian Studies*, 53(1), 123–142.

⚖ Legal Documents, Cases & Government Acts:

- The Constitution (93rd Amendment) Act, 2005. Government of India.
- The Constitution (104th Amendment) Act, 2019. Government of India.
- Report of the Backward Classes Commission (Mandal Commission Report), 1990.
- *T.M.A. Pai Foundation v. State of Karnataka*, (2002) 8 SCC 481.
- *V.P. Nanjundan v. Union of India*, (2001) 8 SCC 208.
- *Bhagwan Das v. Union of India*, AIR 1995 SC 1250.
- The Poona Pact (1932). Agreement between B. R. Ambedkar and M. K. Gandhi.

🌐 Articles, Media & Web Resources:

- Shukla, A. (n.d.). *What is Religious Diversity in India?* [Source: IndiaTimes/Medium — confirm].
- *Asia Highlights: India's Caste System*. (n.d.). [Web article – add link if available].
- *Burning Questions: Dr. B.R. Ambedkar's Manusmriti Dahan*. (n.d.). The Father of Modern India community. [Web article – confirm platform].
- Chinnappan, C. (2018, Nov 27). *Pariyerum Perumal Is a Fervent Portrayal of Our Caste-Ridden Society*. [Medium or Article link – confirm].
- Fathima, A., & Mondal, S. (n.d.). *Brutal Attack on Two Dalit Teens Exposes Caste Fanaticism Among School Kids in TN*. *The News Minute*. [Add link].